Reforming Education Systems for Inclusion and Equity

Reforming Education Systems for Inclusion and Equity addresses the universal challenge of developing forms of education that make a difference for all children and young people, no matter their characteristics or backgrounds. From renowned author Mel Ainscow, this impactful book offers guidance for developing, implementing, and monitoring policies for inclusion and equity in education systems. Drawing from the author's extensive work across the globe as well as from international research contributions and literature in the field, Ainscow presents a framework to plan a strategy for reform, featuring six key ideas: centre inclusion and equity in educational policies; identify and address contextual barriers; support and encourage the development of all members of the learning environment; strengthen networking amongst schools; engage family and community partners; and provide challenge and support locally. This exciting new book is written for school and system leaders, district administrators, community partners, and policy-makers.

Mel Ainscow is Emeritus Professor of Education at the University of Manchester, Professor of Education at the University of Glasgow, and Adjunct Professor at Queensland University of Technology, Australia. A long-term consultant to UNESCO, he is internationally recognised as an authority on the promotion of inclusion and equity in education.

Reforming Education Systems for Inclusion and Equity

Mel Ainscow

NEW YORK AND LONDON

Designed cover image: Getty Images

First published 2026
by Routledge
605 Third Avenue, New York, NY 10158

and by Routledge
4 Park Square, Milton Park, Abingdon, Oxon, OX14 4RN

Routledge is an imprint of the Taylor & Francis Group, an informa business

© 2026 Mel Ainscow

The right of Mel Ainscow to be identified as author of this work has been asserted in accordance with sections 77 and 78 of the Copyright, Designs and Patents Act 1988.

All rights reserved. No part of this book may be reprinted or reproduced or utilised in any form or by any electronic, mechanical, or other means, now known or hereafter invented, including photocopying and recording, or in any information storage or retrieval system, without permission in writing from the publishers.

Trademark notice: Product or corporate names may be trademarks or registered trademarks, and are used only for identification and explanation without intent to infringe.

ISBN: 9781032824901 (hbk)
ISBN: 9781032818283 (pbk)
ISBN: 9781003504788 (ebk)

DOI: 10.4324/9781003504788

Typeset in Caslon
by KnowledgeWorks Global Ltd.

Contents

Preface		vi
Acknowledgements		xiv
1	Education for All: A Global Agenda	1
2	Every Learner Matters and Matters Equally	15
3	Changing Education Systems	38
4	Inquiring Schools	58
5	Moving Knowledge Around	82
6	Beyond the School Gate	101
7	Providing Support and Challenge	121
8	The Challenge of Sustainability	140
References		167
Index		182

Preface

Changing education systems is difficult. This is true even when the proposed changes are relatively straight forward, such as the introduction of a new set of text books, or a different school timetable. So, why is it so difficult? Is it because those involved are lazy or resistant? On the contrary, the key players, particularly teachers, are usually hard-working and extremely busy doing a job that is both intensive and time-consuming.

We also have to keep in mind, too, that teachers are themselves policy-makers. When they go into the classroom and close the door, for the next hour or so what they choose to do is *the* policy as far as their students are concerned. If a teacher doesn't understand changes that are proposed, or even disagrees with them, they are unlikely to happen.

On top of this are the complexities that surround a teacher's life. In explaining what this involves, the organisational theorist Karl Weick argues that schools should be understood as being 'loosely coupled'. That is to say, they consist of units, processes, actions, and individuals that tend to operate in isolation from one another. He illustrates this by describing an unconventional soccer match in which the field is circular with several goals scattered haphazardly around. Weick explains that players enter and leave the game whenever they want, saying 'that's my goal' as many times as they want. He adds that the entire game takes place on a sloped field and is played as if it makes sense (Weick, 1985).

It follows that *educational change is technically simple but socially complex*. It is relatively easy to present proposals for reform, the challenge is to get those involved at the different levels of an education system to understand, accept, and put them into practice.

All of this is an even greater challenge when the changes that are being proposed require a reconsideration of the beliefs of those involved, as is likely to be the case with the suggestions presented in this book. These may require new thinking regarding children and young people, not least regarding their personal characteristics, and social and cultural backgrounds.

The Agenda

This book should be seen as being complementary to *'Developing Inclusive Schools: Pathways to Success'* (Ainscow, 2024a), which is concerned specifically with the development of practices. Here, my focus is on system reform, guided by the following formulations taken from the UNESCO guidance (2017) that I helped produce:

Inclusion – a process that helps overcome barriers limiting the presence, participation, and achievement of learners.
Equity – ensuring that there is a concern with fairness, such that the education of all learners is seen as having equal importance

With these definitions as my guide, I set out to explore how reforms can make use of differences amongst learners to stimulate developments in thinking and improvements in practices within education systems. This requires changes in the way educational policies are understood and implemented at all levels of an education system – from the classroom to the local district, through to the office of the minister.

In the chapters that follow I reflect on over 30 years of developments and research in the United Kingdom and internationally to propose a radical new way of addressing this challenge. This requires a move away from explanations of educational failure that concentrate on the characteristics of individual children and their families, towards an analysis of contextual barriers to participation and learning experienced by students within schools. In this way, those learners who do not respond to existing arrangements come to be regarded as 'hidden voices' who, under certain conditions, can inform the improvement of schools.

This thinking calls for coordinated and sustained efforts within schools and across education systems, recognising that improving outcomes for vulnerable learners is unlikely to be achieved unless there are changes in the attitudes, beliefs, and actions of adults. The starting point must therefore be with policy-makers and practitioners: enlarging their capacity to imagine what might be achieved and increasing their sense of accountability for bringing this about. This may involve tackling negative assumptions, most often relating to expectations about certain groups of students, their capabilities, and behaviours. All of which echoes Michael Fullan's remark: *'If you want system change you have to change the system!'* (Fullan, 2021, p. 36).

Chapter Outlines

Keeping all of this in mind, the book has eight chapters, as follows:

Chapter 1, Education for All: A Global Agenda, provides a summary of international developments over the last thirty years or so. It is explained that the year 2015 was particularly important as a result of commitments made in the form of 17 Sustainable Development Goals, adopted by all United Nations Member States. Sustainable Development Goal 4 aims to *'ensure inclusive and equitable quality education for all'*. This led to the publication of the Education 2030 Framework for Action, which emphasises inclusion and equity as laying the foundations for quality education. It is argued that progress in relation to inclusion and equity requires an effective strategy for implementation. This involves new thinking that focuses attention on the *barriers* experienced by some children that lead them to become marginalised as a result of contextual factors, such as inappropriate curricula and forms of assessment, and inadequate teacher preparation and support. The implication is that addressing such barriers is the most important means of developing forms of education that are effective for all children. In this way, the focus on inclusion and equity becomes a way of achieving the overall improvement of education systems. The chapter also begins a discussion of the roles of research and researchers in relation to this challenging agenda.

Chapter 2, Every Learner Matters and Matters Equally, points to the importance of terminology when trying to change education systems. In particular, terms such as 'equity' and 'inclusion' can be confusing since they may mean different things to different people. This is a particular challenge in relation to national policies, since there is a wide variety of definitions, no clear distinction between the concepts, and an overlap between the definitions of equity and inclusion. This then creates difficulties when trying to move forward with other people – not least in schools, where everybody is so busy. If there is not a shared understanding of the intended direction of travel, progress will be difficult. Therefore, there is a need for agreed definitions of these concepts. In particular, inclusion and equity have to be seen as principles that support and welcome diversity amongst all learners. This presumes that the aim is to eliminate social exclusion that is a consequence of attitudes and responses to diversity in race, social class, ethnicity, religion, gender, and ability. This means that in an education system based on inclusion and equity, all students should be assessed on an on-going basis in relation to their progress. This can be facilitated by the creation of schools that are self-improving.

Chapter 3, Changing Education Systems, describes a series of system change initiatives that occurred over the last three decades in various parts of the United Kingdom. These have included large-scale developments and smaller area-based projects, in contexts where inclusion and equity are a particular challenge. Together these experiences point to the importance of local factors in determining ways of moving thinking and practice forward. In particular, they illustrate the importance of identifying and addressing contextual barriers that limit the presence, participation, and achievement of some learners. The chapter goes on to outline the nature of the obstacles that are likely to be experienced when attempts are made to reform education systems in relation to inclusion and equity. Broadly stated, these relate to: *social factors*, including the extent to which relationships exist that encourage the sharing of expertise through mutual support and challenge; *political factors*, due to the impact of the attitudes and preferences of key partners; and *cultural factors*, created by local traditions and the expectations of those involved as to what is possible. Informed by these arguments, the ideas presented in this book point to the power of education when stakeholders act on their insider knowledge, harnessing local resources to develop coordinated and strategic actions. It is argued that a political mandate is an important factor in making this happen, as is the use of terminology that helps busy colleagues to articulate to one another a sense of common purpose.

Chapter 4, Inquiring Schools, explores how inclusive practices can be developed, the forms of organisation that are required to support such efforts, and the implications for teacher development and leadership practices. It argues that progress is more likely to be successful in contexts where there is a culture of collaboration that encourages and supports problem-solving. According to this view, the development of inclusive practices is seen as involving those within a particular context in working together to address barriers to education experienced by some learners. It is argued that the cultural change necessary to achieve this in schools is a profound one. Traditional school cultures, supported by rigid organisational arrangements, teacher isolation, and high levels of specialisms amongst staff who are geared to predetermined tasks, are often in trouble when faced with unexpected circumstances. On the other hand, the presence of children who are not suited to the existing 'menu' of a school provides some encouragement to explore a more collegiate culture within which teachers are supported in experimenting with new teaching responses. In this way, problem-solving activities may gradually become the reality-defining, taken-for-granted functions that are the culture of an inquiring school.

Chapter 5, Moving Knowledge Around, draws on the findings of studies which indicate that collaboration between schools has an enormous potential for fostering the capacity of education systems to respond to learner diversity. More specifically, this research shows how such partnerships can help reduce the polarisation of schools within an education system, to the particular benefit of those students who are marginalised at the edges of the system, and whose performance and attitudes cause concern. There is also evidence that when schools seek to develop more collaborative ways of working, this can have an impact on how teachers perceive themselves and their work. Specifically, comparisons of practices in different schools can lead practitioners to view underachieving students in a new light. In this way, learners who cannot easily be educated within a school's established routines come to be seen less as 'having problems' but as challenging teachers to re-examine their practices in order to make them more responsive and flexible. The chapter considers the particular challenges of implementing this thinking within those countries where there is an increased policy emphasis on school autonomy, competition between schools, and parental choice. Focusing on examples of area partnerships that proved to be effective, it is explained that these were guided by a strong commitment to equity, underpinned by context-informed decision-making at the local level.

Chapter 6, Beyond the School Gate, argues that progress towards the development of education systems that are effective for all children and young people will only happen when what happens outside as well as inside a school changes. Indeed, there is encouraging evidence of what can happen when what schools do is aligned in a coherent strategy with the efforts of other community players: families, employers, community groups, universities, and public services. The chapter argues that this does not necessarily mean schools doing more, but it does imply partnerships beyond the school, where partners multiply the impacts of each other's efforts. However, experience suggests that the success of such partnerships is dependent upon a common understanding of what they are trying to achieve and an engagement with various forms of evidence to stimulate collective effort. Examples of place-based developments are analysed in order to draw lessons that can be used to guide the planning of such initiatives. All of this has implications for the various key stakeholders within education systems. In particular, teachers, especially those in senior positions, have to see themselves as having a wider responsibility for all children, not just those who attend their own schools. They also have to develop patterns of internal organisation that enable them to have the flexibility to cooperate with stakeholders beyond the school gate.

Chapter 7, Providing Support and Challenge, considers what it is that those at a local district level can contribute to efforts to promote inclusion and equity across an education system. It is argued that district-level staff can have an important role to play, not least in acting as the 'conscience of the system' – making sure that all children and young people are getting a fair deal within an increasingly diverse system of education. In order to do this, they need to have the big picture about what is happening in their communities, identifying priorities for action and brokering collaboration. In such contexts, those involved come to value differences, believe in collaboration, and are committed to offering educational opportunities to all students. However, changing the cultural norms that exist within an area education system is difficult to achieve. Therefore, leaders at the local level, including those in civil society and other sectors, have to be prepared to analyse their own situations, identify local barriers and facilitators, plan an appropriate development process, and provide support for inclusive practices and effective strategies for monitoring equity in education. Within these locally coordinated developments, the presence of experienced advisers who are able to support and challenge school-led improvement is crucial.

And finally, **Chapter 8, The Challenge of Sustainability,** draws together six propositions developed in the book in order to create a framework that can be used to guide developments for promoting inclusion and equity within educational systems. It reports on an on-going system reform project in order to explore the organisational conditions that are needed in order to foster such developments and the forms of leadership that are needed in order to make this happen. These suggestions are based on the idea that schools and their communities have untapped potential to improve their capacity for improving the presence, participation, and achievement of all of their students, particularly those who are vulnerable to marginalisation or exclusion. The challenge therefore is to mobilise this potential in order to achieve changes that are sustainable. This reinforces the argument that educational improvement is a social process that involves practitioners in learning from one another, from their students, and from others involved in the lives of the young people they teach. At the same time, it is necessary to address contextual barriers that may prevent reforms from occurring in order to achieve sustainable change. The chapter concludes by discussing the implications for the stances, roles, and methodologies of those in the research community.

Throughout the chapters I stress the need to recognise that context matters. This means that what works in one place may not work in another. Sensitive implementation is therefore essential. Bearing this in mind, the suggestions I present are not intended as prescriptions to be simply lifted and re-used. Rather, they are ideas that have to be adapted to fit particular circumstances.

Acknowledgements

It is in the nature of a book like this that many colleagues have contributed to the ideas that are presented. Wherever possible, these contributions are signalled using references in the text.

In four of the chapters, I have drawn more specifically on work carried out in partnership with colleagues. These are: in Chapter 4, Kiki Messiou; and Ignacio Calderón-Almendros, Cynthia Duk, and Mercedes Viola; in Chapter 5, Paul Armstrong, Bee Hughes, and Stephen Rayner; in Chapter 6, Kirstin Kerr; and in Chapter 8, Chris Chapman and our colleagues at the University of Glasgow. I thank all these partners and many more who have helped me along the way.

Finally, I owe particular thanks to five internationally recognised scholars: Alan Dyson, Michael Fullan (who suggested that I should write this book), Andy Hargreaves, David Hargreaves, and Karen Seashore Louis. Over many years, they have inspired, encouraged, and supported me. Their willingness to give their time to colleagues is something I admire and try to emulate.

1
EDUCATION FOR ALL
A GLOBAL AGENDA

Achieving inclusion and equity is a challenge facing education systems throughout the world. Put simply, the concern is to find ways of ensuring that all children and young people are included in schools and treated as being of equal importance. In this book, I explore what can be done to promote this agenda within education systems, focusing on the following questions:

- How can education systems promote inclusion and equity?
- What are the barriers and how might they be overcome?
- What should be the roles of research and researchers?

In addressing this agenda, I draw on the experience of system change initiatives that took place in the United Kingdom over the last 30 years, plus developments in a variety of other countries. This leads me to develop a series of propositions that may be relevant to the development of strategies to other contexts. First of all, however, I begin by summarising relevant international developments, to some of which I have made contributions (Ainscow, 2024b).

A Global Challenge

Since 1990, the United Nation's Education for All (EFA) movement has worked to make quality basic education available to all learners. The EFA Declaration sets out an overall vision, which is about being proactive in identifying the barriers some learners encounter in attempting to access educational opportunities. This also involves the identification of resources available at national and community levels, and bringing them to bear on overcoming those barriers.

This vision was reaffirmed by the World Education Forum meeting in Dakar, 2000, held to review the progress made during the previous decade. The Forum declared that EFA must take particular account of the needs of the poor and the disadvantaged, including working children, remote rural dwellers and nomads, and ethnic and linguistic minorities, young people affected by conflict, HIV/AIDS, hunger, and poor health, and those with special learning needs.

A major impetus for this inclusive emphasis was given by the World Conference on Special Needs Education in 1994, during which more than 300 participants, representing 92 governments and 25 international organisations, met in Salamanca, Spain. The purpose of the conference was to further the objective of EFA by considering the fundamental policy shifts required to promote the approach of inclusive education, namely, enabling schools to serve all children, particularly those defined as having special educational needs (Ainscow, 2024b).

The movement towards inclusive education was further strengthened by the 48th session of the IBE-UNESCO International Conference on Education held in 2008, with its theme *'Inclusive Education: The Way of the Future'* (Opertti, Walker and Zhang, 2014). The long-term objective of this event was to support UNESCO member states in providing the social and political conditions which every person needs in order to exercise their human right to access, take an active part in, and benefit from educational opportunities.

During this event, ministers and government officials from around the world, plus representatives of voluntary organisations, discussed the importance of broadening the concept of inclusion to focus on all children, under the assumption that every learner matters equally and has the right to receive effective educational opportunities. This involves radical thinking in the field regarding the idea of inclusive education. It argues that the aim is to eliminate social exclusion that is a consequence of attitudes and responses to diversity in race, social class, ethnicity, religion, gender, and ability. As such, it represents a challenge to existing thinking regarding the development of education systems.

The Current Situation

Despite these developments, a Global Monitoring Report pointed out that an estimated 258 million children and young people are still not in school (UNESCO, 2020). Furthermore, the UNESCO Institute for Statistics data show that more than 617 million children and adolescents are not achieving minimum proficiency levels in reading and mathematics (UIS, 2019). Meanwhile, the OECD reports that the poorest learners, living in the poorest areas, achieve less well than their wealthier peers, with these patterns found across higher and lower-income countries. It also found that race, gender, and a host of other factors, intersect and deepen these entrenched economic and spatial inequities (OECD, 2021). Adding to this, UNICEF (2022) reports that, globally, nearly two-thirds of 10-year-olds are unable to read and understand simple text.

A report from the European Commission (2020) reflected on the prevalence of similar patterns of educational inequity across its 27 member states. It reached the damning verdict that, *'Education is failing to reduce inequalities linked to socio-economic status, despite the fact that the highest performing national education systems are those that put a premium on equity'* (para 2.2).

The year 2015 was particularly important in relation to these challenges. Commitments were made in the form of 17 Sustainable Development Goals, adopted by all United Nations Member States. Sustainable Development Goal 4 aims to *'ensure inclusive and equitable quality education for all'*. This led to the publication of the Education 2030 Framework for Action, which emphasises inclusion and equity as laying the foundations for quality education (UNESCO, 2015).

The introduction of the concept of equity into these international policy debates was significant in that it points to the importance of fairness, leading to the need to address all forms of exclusion and marginalisation, disparities and inequalities in access, participation, and learning processes and outcomes. In this way, it was made clear that the international EFA agenda really has to be about *'all'*.

Like all major policy changes, progress in relation to inclusion and equity requires an effective strategy for implementation. For me, this must involve new thinking that focuses attention on the barriers experienced by some children that lead them to become marginalised as a result of contextual factors, such as inappropriate curricula and forms of assessment, and inadequate teacher preparation and support. The implication is that addressing such barriers is the most important means of developing forms of education that are effective for all children. In this way, the focus on inclusion and equity provides a way of achieving the overall improvement of education systems.

In support of these global developments in 2017, I led the development for UNESCO of its *Guide for Ensuring Inclusion and Equity in Education*. This guide offers practical support to Member States to help review how well equity and inclusion currently figure in existing policies, decide what actions need to be taken to improve policies, and monitor progress as actions are taken. The document focuses on the following definitions:

Inclusion – a process that helps overcome barriers limiting the presence, participation, and achievement of learners.
Equity – ensuring that there is a concern with fairness, such that the education of all learners is seen as having equal importance.

The UNESCO guide goes on to present a principle that has subsequently been influential internationally and is central to the thinking put forward in this book: *Every Learner Matters and Matters Equally*.

Promising Developments

The situation across the world in relation to this challenging policy agenda is complex, with some countries making great strides, whilst others continue to have segregated provision of various forms for some groups of learners. There are, however, countries where there has been encouraging progress, such as:

- The **Italian** government passed a law in 1977 that closed all special schools, units, and other non-inclusive forms of provision (Ianes, Demo and Dell'Anna, 2020) This legislation is still in force and more recent amendments have further strengthened the inclusive nature of the education system. Not only did this close segregated educational facilities but, starting with pre-schools, it removed the possibility of exclusion from school as a corrective sanction. Whilst practice varies from place to place, the principle of inclusion is widely accepted. There are, however, concerns about students being withdrawn for periods outside the regular classroom for additional support.

- For more than 30 years, the province of New Brunswick in Canada has pioneered the concept of inclusive education through legislation, local authority policies, and professional guidelines (AuCoin, Porter and Baker-Korotkov, 2020) More recently, New Brunswick adopted a policy which defines the critical elements of an inclusive education system that supports students in common learning environments and provides support for teachers. It sets clear requirements for school practice including procedures for the development of personalised learning plans, inclusive graduation, as well as strict guidelines when a variation of the common learning environment may be required.

- An inclusive education policy has led to significant progress in Sierra Leone, with more children enroled in schools than ever before, particularly girls.[1] In early 2021, Sierra Leone approved its first-ever policy on inclusive education, the National Policy on Radical Inclusion in schools. This policy seeks to increase enrolment, retention, and successful transition of all students in pre-primary, primary, and senior secondary education, regardless of disability, gender, pregnancy or parenting status, geographic location, and socio-economic background.

- Having enacted legislation making disability discrimination within education unlawful, Portugal has gone much further in enacting an explicit legal framework for the inclusion of all students in education (Alves, Campos Pinto and Pinto, 2020). Recent legislation requires that the provision of support be determined, managed, and provided at the regular school level, with local multidisciplinary teams responsible for determining what support is necessary to ensure all students have access and the means to participate effectively in education, with a view to their full inclusion in society. It is also significant that Portugal has developed progressive assessment practices to support the achievement of all learners. As the Portuguese education system moved forward in relation to inclusion over the last two decades, the country has also seen impressive developments in terms of equity (OECD, 2022). It is also one of the few countries with a positive trajectory of improvement in all of the subjects assessed by OECD's Programme for International Student Assessment (PISA).

- Vietnam provides an illustration of how education provision can improve at a larger scale, even in a country with a developing economy and over 15 million students.[2] The majority of the Vietnamese population (nearly 86%) are from the Kinh ethnic group, but there are 53 other ethnic groups. Some of these groups have long had high levels of literacy and education but the Vietnamese government has also made a concerted effort to support the education of students from ethnic minority groups who live in rural areas, mountainous, and remote regions, and who experience higher levels of poverty. These efforts have contributed to near universal access to education at a relatively high level of quality. This has been achieved through an emphasis on collective action. This includes close coordination between authorities at grassroots levels and schools.

- In Finland, a country which has regularly outperformed most other countries in terms of educational outcomes, education is viewed as a right and not as a privilege. The country's success is partly explained by the progress of the lowest performing quintile of students who outperform those in other countries (Sabel et al., 2011). This has increasingly involved an emphasis on support for vulnerable students within mainstream schools, as opposed to in segregated provision. There is a particular focus on prevention of learning difficulties in Finland, and a high level of resources are directed at this in primary schools. For example, all Finnish schools are assigned specialists to support any student who requires additional help.

Further encouragement regarding inclusion and equity is provided by the 'Report Card' prepared for UNICEF by the UNICEF (2018), which concludes:

> Tackling educational inequality does not mean sacrificing high standards. Countries with higher average achievement tend to have lower levels of inequality.... Bringing the worst performing students up does not mean pulling the best-performing students down.
>
> (p. 3)

This Report Card focuses on educational inequalities in 41 of the world's richest countries, all of which are members of the Organisation for Economic Co-operation and Development and/or the European Union. It argues that there is no systematic relationship between country income and indicators of equality in education. For example, it is notable that some of the economically poorer countries in the comparison, such as Latvia and Lithuania, achieve near-universal access to pre-school learning and curb inequality in reading performance among both primary and secondary school students more successfully than countries that have far greater resources. The Report Card concludes that Finland, Latvia, and Portugal have the most equal education systems.

In drawing attention to these examples of policy development, I stress that they should not be seen as being perfect. Rather, they are countries where there are interesting developments from which to learn. They are also varied with respect to the approaches used and what they have achieved. To take an example, some writers have recently suggested that care should be taken not to overestimate the progress made with regard to inclusive education in Canada.[3] Consequently, whilst lessons can undoubtedly be learned from these developments, they must be replicated with care.

It is also important to keep in mind that there are many sources of inequity in education related to political, economic, social, cultural, and institutional factors, and that these vary across countries. This means that what works in one country may not work elsewhere. An emphasis on system change strategies being contextually sensitive is a pervading theme of the recommendations made in this book.

Other Global Trends

In some countries, increasing pressures to improve the rankings of education systems on global league tables is creating new barriers to progress in relation to inclusion and equity. This arises because of an increased emphasis on school autonomy, competition between schools, and parental choice (Meyland-Smith & Evans, 2009). The schools involved have different titles, such as charter schools in the USA, free schools in Sweden, academies in England, and independent public schools in parts of Australia. Implicit in these independent state-funded schools is an assumption that greater autonomy will allow space for the development of organisational arrangements, practices, and forms of management and leadership that will be more effective in promoting the learning of all students, particularly those from economically disadvantaged and minority backgrounds.

In later chapters, I return to this global trend and the varied views that exist as to the extent to which it is leading to the desired outcomes. In particular, there is a concern that the development of education systems based on autonomy, coupled with high-stakes accountability and increased competition between schools, will further disadvantage learners from low-income and minority families (Salokangas and Ainscow, 2017). For example, parental choice and competition between schools have widened the gap between schools that are seen to be more successful and those that are perceived to be less so in countries as varied as Chile, England, Sweden and the United States.

Meanwhile, the New Zealand Government published a policy document based on the findings of a review carried by an independent task force (Ministry of Education, 2019). This concluded that a key reason for the country's poor equity and achievement outcomes is that, since reforms were introduced in 1989, schools had predominantly operated as autonomous, self-managing entities, loosely connected to each other and with a distant relationship with the centre. This autonomy left schools to operate largely on their own and without sufficient support. The document outlines the Government's strategy for the reform of the schooling system. This involves a move towards a networked system that is more responsive to the needs of all learners, an approach I recommend later in this book. However, in a way that illustrates how national policies can change direction quickly, in May 2024 an announcement was made that up to 50 new or converted charter schools will be funded.[4]

In relation to these trends, the OECD (2012) reports the success of education systems that rank highly on measures of both quality and equity. As a result, it argues:

> The evidence is conclusive: equity in education pays off. The highest performing education systems across OECD countries are those that combine high quality and equity. In such education systems, the vast majority of students can attain high level skills and knowledge that depend on their ability and drive, more than on their socio-economic background.
>
> (p. 14)

The implication, then, is that it is possible for countries to develop education systems that are both equitable and excellent. Indeed, my argument is that equity can provide a pathway to excellence. The question is: how can this be achieved? Broadly stated, this is the agenda I address in this book.

Research and Policy-Making

Taking account of this international policy agenda, the chapters that follow argue that effective educational reform requires the coming together of processes of social learning and collaborative action within settings that stretch from multiple classrooms to the committee rooms of senior policy-makers. This leads me to argue that research and researchers can have helpful roles in facilitating such processes. However, this means that in order to contribute, researchers have to develop new skills in creating collaborative partnerships that cross borders between actors who have different professional experiences (Ainscow, Chapman and Hadfield, 2020). As I will show, this is a messy rather than linear process. Subsequent chapters illustrate how the different roles and sociocultural contexts of policy-makers/practitioners and academics create a complex set of power relations, which have to be factored into processes as simple as introducing ideas from research to the complexities of co-producing knowledge and joint action.

Reimers and McGinn (1997) argue that education systems are *'arenas of conflict'*, rather than machines, and what they do is a reflection of how different actors within a system construct their roles. In this book, I draw on my privileged position as a researcher who has worked across such arenas of conflict through my involvement in a series of improvement programmes in the United Kingdom and various other countries across the world. This leads me to offer advice on how research and, indeed, researchers can best contribute to improvements in the field. In so doing, I argue that education systems will only be able to use research effectively if steps are taken to overcome locally specific social, political, and cultural barriers. As I will explain, this analysis has implications for policy-makers, practitioners and, indeed, for those of us working in the world of academic research.

Much has been written about the relationship between research and policy, some of which have focused on the quality of educational research itself. For example, almost 20 years ago, Whitty (2006) summarised what he saw as the 'abuse of educational research'. While much has changed since this was written, such perceptions remain as strong as ever. However, for the purposes of this book, I put issues about the quality of the research to one side in order to focus on two key sets of relationships: between research and policy-making, and, just as significantly, between researchers and practitioners.

Some of the literature sets up divisions between those involved in the production of research and those involved in the construction of policies in public services (e.g., Innvaer et al., 2002). This sees researchers as adopting a traditional stance – that of the interested spectator, gathering evidence and finding ways of feeding their findings into the field of play. With colleagues I have adopted a radically different stance, that of the *engaged researcher*, working alongside policy-makers and practitioners in the field, trying to use our research-based knowledge to inform decision-making as it occurs (Ainscow, Chapman and Hadfeld, 2020). Being an engaged researcher, embedded within government policy-making but also working alongside practitioners as they reconstruct policy at different levels of an education system, not least the level of the school, is a difficult stance to adopt. The analysis I provide in subsequent chapters throws some light on the nature of these difficulties and how they can be overcome.

Influencing Policy-Making

With regard to education policy-making, the uptake of research findings often remains limited. For example, Harris et al. (2013) argue that despite a valid knowledge base about what works and why at classroom, school, and increasingly system levels, policy-making communities have been reluctant to engage with research findings, and when they have this has tended to be selective. This can lead to situations where political ideology, anecdote and, on occasion, whim dominate policy-making.

The lack of evidence-based policy-making in national education systems has been explained in terms of communication, institutional, and cultural gaps between researchers and policy-makers (Mitton et al., 2007). Such gaps can have an adverse effect, leading to professional divides, suspicion, and mistrust that become mutually reinforcing in ways that create a downward spiral that further minimises research influence on policy-making.

Policy change in education usually involves a process of complex negotiation between competing interests. This is another explanation for the paucity of research utilisation within the policy-making process (Reimers and McGinn, 1997). Levin (2011) provides a helpful practical model to consider how knowledge mobilisation occurs, using three interconnected contexts: production, use, and mediation. These contexts are not necessarily structures. Rather, they are better thought of as functions, with some people, organisations, or groups operating in one or more of the contexts.

Those that attempt to move between research and policy communities operate across all three contexts. Sullivan and Skeltcher (2002) refer to such individuals as 'reticulists' who build capacity and collaborative practices to enhance their influence. They tend to be:

- *Skilled communicators* – with the ability to adapt their language to specific settings and empathise with others, through negotiation and seeing a situation from a range of perspectives.
- *Networkers* – gaining access to a range of settings, seeking out and connecting with others with common interests and goals.

- *Strategic in orientation* – they see the 'big picture' and understand how different partners can contribute to achieve common goals.
- *Contextually astute* – they understand how opportunities and constraints within the organisation can influence individual's behaviour.
- *Problem-solvers* – they think laterally and creatively to seek solutions to the challenges they face.
- *Self-managing* – they take risks within a framework that understands organisational capacity. In this sense, they have sound organisational skills.

Even with such qualities, however, the challenge of knowledge mobilisation and research uptake remains a complex process involving varied influences, from the motivation and skills of decision-makers to the ability of researchers to effect decision-making structures and processes. A sense of what this can mean was well illustrated by David Laws, a former Schools' Minister in the UK Government, who commented:

> A lot of decision-making is not based on evidence but on hunch. I had little coming to me from civil servants that presented the latest academic evidence. Too often, they just serve up practical advice about how the minister can do what he or she wants. But politicians are prone to make decisions based on ideology and personal experience.
> (Ainscow, Chapman and Hadfield, 2020)

This highlights graphically some of the challenges faced by researchers working in the spaces between research and policy-making/practitioner communities. With this in mind, in the chapters that follow I explain my experiences of attempting to navigate these spaces within various education systems.

Context Matters

As noted above, the idea that system change strategies have to be contextually sensitive is one of the pervading themes of the suggestions I make in this book. A recent UNESCO report on developments in Ghana provides a vivid example of why this is so vital.[5]

It points out that the majority of the educational problems children in that country face can be traced to local experiences that disrupt their learning process. Moreover, these problems are mostly micro-level experiences related to language differences in the classroom, gender roles in children's lives, and tensions between school and farm work. And, of course, all of this has major implications for policy decisions that focus on achieving equity.

To throw further light on what this means for the sorts of experiences I draw on in this book, I return to a study published over 25 years ago, in which my colleague Tony Booth and I analysed the perspectives on inclusion (and exclusion) revealed by teams of researchers in their accounts of schools in eight countries (Booth and Ainscow 1998). The study arose from our dissatisfaction with much of the existing comparative education research, which seeks findings that will have global significance by oversimplifying educational processes and practices, and by ignoring problems of interpretation and translation. We were also concerned about studies that assumed the existence of a single national perspective, rather than reporting the conflicts of interest and points of view that arise in all countries. In these ways, we argued that important differences between and within countries are too often omitted from study and debate.

Given these concerns, Booth and I intended that our study of developments in the eight countries would enhance interest in the shaping effect of national and local policies, as well as cultural and linguistic histories, on educational practice. It would do this, we hoped, by extending existing comparative reviews of inclusion through making their viewpoints explicit and illustrating practice in all its messiness. We also set out to challenge the way notions of inclusive education are often interpreted through the narrow, deficit lens of traditional special education thinking.

We went on to argue that an awareness of viewpoint diversity would avoid two pitfalls of comparative research: the idea that, in any country, there is a single national perspective on inclusion; and the notion that practice can be generalised across countries without attention to local contexts and meanings. The tendency to present single national perspectives, we explained, is often matched by a failure to describe the way practice is to be understood in its local and national context.

This is part of a positivist view of social science, in which research carried out in one country can be amalgamated with that of others in order to support generalisable conclusions.

All of this is in marked contrast to the experiences I refer to in this book. These accounts attempt to draw out nuances of the meaning of policy and practice in particular places. In many instances, this means listening directly to the voices of those involved, not least those of children and young people and their families. Rather than reducing the potential contribution of research conducted in unfamiliar contexts, I suggest that a careful analysis of these differences in perspective, context, and meaning enhances their value.

Conclusion

In this first chapter, I have explained the global interest in developing education systems that can address the challenge of inclusion and equity. I have also begun a discussion of the roles of research and researchers in relation to this challenging agenda.

The chapters that follow explore these ideas further in order to develop six propositions that are, I believe, relevant to those concerned with addressing this reform agenda within their contexts. This analysis also throws light on the challenges that can be experienced when putting this thinking into practice.

Notes

1 https://education-profiles.org/sub-saharan-africa/sierra-leone/~inclusion
2 buff.ly/44MZ9IZ
3 For example: file:///Users/melainscow/Desktop/Paul%20W.%20Bennett:%20Inclusive%20education%20is%20an%20illusion%20in%20post-pandemic%20schools.%20Too%20often,%20it%E2%80%99s%20simply.html
4 https://www.odt.co.nz/news/national/govt-give-153m-charter-schools
5 https://world-education-blog.org/2024/06/04/understanding-learning-disparities-in-ghanas-basic-school-system-implications-for-achieving-learning-equity/

2
EVERY LEARNER MATTERS AND MATTERS EQUALLY

Having summarised global trends, in this chapter, I go on to trace the development of the thinking that informs the approach to system reform presented in this book. This has occurred as a result of my involvement in a series of development and research projects over the last 30 years or so. Running through these activities, all of which have involved collaboration with partners in the field, is my own professional journey.

Over many years, my work has been related to a variety of headline themes, starting from special education, through to integration, on to inclusive education, and then educational equity (see Ainscow, 2016a, for a more detailed account of this process). A pattern emerges from these developments. They have involved periods of uncertainty as my thinking was challenged by new experiences and different contexts, through a process I describe as 'making the familiar unfamiliar'. What also becomes evident is the way that working with colleagues has helped me to cope with these disturbances, such that they often became critical incidents that led to developments in my ideas.

Shifting Perspectives

After some years working as a secondary school art teacher, and then as a teacher and headteacher in special schools, in 1979 I took up the post of Adviser for Special Needs for the Coventry local authority, in England. This move opened up splendid new opportunities for me to reposition myself and to take my thinking forward. In so doing, it began my interest in school improvement and educational change.

Alongside my specialism, the role included providing general advice on school development matters to a group of primary and secondary schools. For somebody who had spent so much time working in special provision, this presented new challenges. In particular, it opened up opportunities to explore how schools can develop ways of working that promote the integration of children who might otherwise be placed in special provision.

At that time, the Coventry authority had a strong commitment to encouraging innovation in its schools and to providing professional development for teachers in order to encourage improvements in practice. As I contributed to these developments, I formulated a proposal for a large-scale initiative to promote integration across the authority's schools. Working with a committed and innovative educational psychologist, Jim Muncey, we designed what came to be known as the Special Needs Action Programme (SNAP) – a detailed account of this is provided in Ainscow and Muncey (1989). In order to take SNAP forward, we asked each school to designate a member of staff as their special needs coordinator, somebody who could act as the lead for developments across the staff. Later this approach became part of national policy in England and was to influence developments in many other parts of world. Linked to this, our mantra was 'every teacher a special needs teacher'.

The initial phase of SNAP concentrated on primary schools. The core activity was based around a set of staff development resources called 'Small Steps', which involved helping teachers to design the sorts of individualised learning programmes that I had previously used in special schools (see Ainscow and Tweddle, 1979, 1984). In addition, further staff development packages were developed, including one that focused on ways of addressing difficulties in student behaviour and others that focused on issues to do with various learner impairments.

Eventually, the decision was made to extend SNAP into the secondary sector. With this in mind, Muncey and I formed a working group of experienced teachers to help us formulate a way forward. Discussions in this group led to a period of personal turbulence for me, as it became clear that the sorts of individualised approach that I had used in the primary sector would not be feasible in secondary schools. However, the debate went beyond a consideration of practicalities, leading to a major rethink of my orientation.

In many ways, this period represented the most important turning point in my career. It involved me in moving away from a narrow concern with individual learners, deemed to be vulnerable, to a focus on the wider contexts in which learning takes place. As a result, the SNAP staff development package for the secondary sector shifted the agenda to a consideration of many aspects of a school's work, i.e., the curriculum, teaching practices, management and leadership, monitoring of student progress, and support for learning. Later, I realised that this was pushing me to reposition my work as being about school improvement and system reform.

Moving Forward

Developments in my thinking about educational change were further stimulated when I took up a post at the University of Cambridge Institute of Education. This led to the 'Improving the Quality of Education for All' (IQEA) project, which David Hopkins and I instigated in the early 1990s.

Initially, this involved us in working with a small number of schools in and around London (Ainscow and Hopkins, 1992). Subsequently, it led to developments in other parts of the world, including Hong Kong, Iceland, and Puerto Rica (see Ainscow, 1999; Clarke et al., 2006; Hopkins, 2007; Hopkins et al., 1994; West and Ainscow, 2010 for more detailed accounts of some of these projects). All of these initiatives involved teams of researchers working in partnership with networks of schools to identify ways in which the learning of all members of a school community – students, parents, and staff – could be enhanced.

Work with schools in the IQEA projects was based upon a contract that attempted to define the parameters for our involvement and the obligations those involved owed to one another. This emphasised that all staff should be consulted; that an in-school team of coordinators be appointed to carry the work forward; that a critical mass of staff were to be actively involved; and that sufficient time would be made available for necessary classroom and staff development activities. Meanwhile, we committed ourselves to supporting school developments, usually in the first place for one year. Often the arrangement continued, however, and in some instances, we were involved for periods as long as seven years. We provided training for the school coordinators, made regular school visits, and contributed to school-based staff development activities. In addition, we attempted to work with the schools in recording and analysing their experiences in a way that also provided data relevant to our own on-going research agenda.

As a result of engagements with schools involved in the IQEA project, we evolved a style of collaboration that was to influence later initiatives, which we referred to as *'working with, rather than working on'* (Ainscow and Southworth, 1996). This phrase attempted to sum up an approach that deliberately allowed each project school considerable autonomy to determine its own priorities for development and, indeed, its methods for achieving these priorities. In attempting to work in this way, we found ourselves confronted with staggering complexity, and by a bewildering array of policy and strategy options. It was our belief, however, that only through a regular engagement with these complexities could a greater understanding of school change be achieved.

Further Research

In the light of these experiences, I have subsequently found it essential to engage in forms of research that are to a large degree located within schools and classrooms and that require me to work in partnership with teachers. The overall aim of this approach is to understand difficulties experienced in schools from the points of view of insiders and to explore together how these can be addressed in ways that attempt to support the growth of those involved.

My thinking about all of this was much influenced as a result of the development of the 'Index for Inclusion' (Booth and Ainscow, 2000). Designed by a team of activists for use within the policy context of England at the turn of the century, the Index is a set of school review materials that have been refined as a result of over ten years of collaborative action research in many countries. It is now available in more than 40 languages and is widely used internationally[1].

The Index enables schools to draw on the resources of staff, students, parents/carers, and community representatives in order to address barriers to the participation and learning of students that exist within their existing 'cultures, policies and practices'. In connecting inclusion with the details of policy as it is implemented in particular contexts, the Index encourages those who use it to build up their own view of inclusion, related to their experience and values, as they work out what policies and practices they wish to promote or discourage. Such an approach is based on the idea that inclusion is essentially about attempts to embody particular values within specific contexts. In other words, it involves 'school improvement with attitude' (Ainscow et al., 2006).

The Index approach requires coordinated and sustained efforts around the idea that changing outcomes for all students is unlikely to be achieved unless there are changes in the behaviours of adults. Consequently, the starting point for inclusive school development is with teachers: in effect, enlarging their capacity to imagine what might be achieved, and increasing their sense of accountability for bringing this about. This may also involve tackling taken-for-granted assumptions, most often relating to expectations about certain groups of students, their capabilities, behaviour, and patterns of attendance. At the same time, such efforts have to be linked to what is happening in other schools and the wider community. Ainscow (2024a) provides accounts of my use of the Index in various countries.

The work on the Index for Inclusion, alongside the findings from our earlier efforts to explore the potential of inquiry-based approaches, influenced the design of a series of further projects when I moved to the University of Manchester, particularly:

- *Understanding and Developing Inclusive Practices in Schools.* This collaborative action research project, which occurred between 2000 and 2004, involved a network of 25 urban schools in three

English local education authorities and three partner universities. Within the network schools, we saw how the use of evidence to study teaching can help to foster the development of more inclusive forms of teaching (see Ainscow et al., 2004, 2006; Howes et al., 2004, 2005).

- *An Equity Research Network.* Between 2006 and 2011 I had a chance to explore these ideas in more detail through our involvement with secondary schools in an English local authority (see Ainscow et al., 2012a, 2012b). This initiative was located in a local authority characterised by socio-economic disadvantage, and social and ethnic segregation. It involved staff inquiry groups in the participating schools, usually consisting of five or six members representing different perspectives within their school communities.
- *Ethical Leadership: A collaborative investigation of equity-driven evidence-based school reform.* This three-year study involved a research network of schools from across the geographically spread State of Queensland, Australia, and a team of eight university researchers from Queensland University of Technology, of which I was a part-time member. Together, we explored how ethical leadership could promote ways of interpreting and using various forms of evidence to promote learning and equity (see: Harris et al., 2017, 2020; Spina et al., 2019).
- *Inclusive Inquiry.* Carried out between 2012 and 2020 in five European countries, this research focused more specifically on how students can themselves contribute to the development of inclusive teaching and learning. It involved the development of 'inclusive inquiry', a strategy in which children and young people becoming researchers who learn how to use inquiry methods to gather the views of their classmates, as well as observing lessons (see: Messiou et al., 2016; Messiou and Ainscow, 2015, 2020; Ainscow and Messiou, 2017).
- *Reaching Out to All Learners.*[2] I coordinated the development of these professional development materials for UNESCO-IBE, working with a team of international experts. This involved field research in Australia, Canada, Chile, India, South Africa, and Spain. The resource pack is intended to influence and support

inclusive thinking and practices at all levels of an education system. It is designed to be relevant to teachers, school leaders, district-level administrators, teacher educators, and national policy-makers. The materials are currently being disseminated globally, with my support, through cooperation with governments and other international organisations.

- *Promoting inclusion and equity in Latin America.* Focusing specifically on finding ways of using professional development to promote developments in Latin America (see Calderón-Almendros et al., 2020), this programme of development and research has involved two phases. The first of these involved participatory research experiences in seven Latin American countries (i.e., Chile, Colombia, Ecuador, Mexico, Paraguay, Peru, and Uruguay), and the second phase took the form of collaborative inquiry projects with networks of schools in some of these countries (Ainscow et al., in press).

All of these studies involved teams of university researchers in supporting, recording, and analysing collaborative action research as it occurred within education systems. As a result, I came to define this as a process of knowledge-generation that occurs when researcher and practitioner knowledge meet in particular sites and is aimed at producing new knowledge about ways in which broad values might better be realised in future practice.

In trying to make sense of the complex processes involved in adopting this stance my colleagues and I have found it helpful to see them in relation to what we have defined as an *'ecology of equity'* (Ainscow et al., 2012a. By) this, I mean that the extent to which students' experiences and outcomes are equitable is not dependent only on the educational practices of their schools. Instead, it depends on a whole range of interacting processes that reach into the school from outside. These include the demographics of the areas served by schools, the histories and cultures of the populations who send (or fail to send) their children to the school, and the economic realities faced by those populations.

This suggests that it is necessary to address three interlinked sets of factors that impact on the learning of students. These relate to: *within-school factors* to do with existing policies and practices; *between-school factors* that arise from the characteristics of local school systems; and *beyond-school factors*, including the demographics, economics, cultures, and histories of local areas. Focusing on these factors can create the conditions for reform.

Intervention Projects

Opportunities to explore how this thinking could be used to promote system-wide change were provided by my involvement in a series of government-instigated initiatives in various parts of the United Kingdom. First of all, between 2004 and 2006, my colleague Andy Howes and I carried out a study on behalf of the government of an improvement process known as 'Transforming Secondary Education' in an English city where the performance of the school system was a cause for considerable concern. The initiative attempted to use collaboration within four networks of secondary schools as the main route to sustainable higher achievement (Ainscow and Howes, 2007).

Our research led us to a positive conclusion about the role that collaboration played in creating pathways for improvement in the city. Over a relatively short period, the schools demonstrated how partnerships can provide an effective means of solving immediate problems, such as staff shortages; how they can have a positive impact during periods of crisis, such as during the closure of a school; and, how, in the longer run, schools working together can contribute to the raising of aspirations and attainment in schools that have had a record of low achievement. Meanwhile, statistical data showed that attainment levels increased in all four groupings. There was also strong evidence that collaboration helped reduce the polarisation of the education system, to the particular benefit of those students who are on the edges of the system and performing relatively poorly, although this impact was uneven.

In the years that followed I had the good fortune to have an active role in a series of further system change initiatives. The largest of these were: City Challenge in England (2003–2011), Schools Challenge Cymru in Wales (2014–2017), and the Central

South Wales Challenge (2014–2017). Each of these initiatives had strong government mandates, plus massive financial and resource investments (see detailed accounts in: Ainscow, 2015, 2020, 2023; Ainscow, Chapman and Hadfield, 2020). More recently, I have worked alongside my colleagues at the University of Glasgow on a series of related developments in Scotland (Chapman and Ainscow, 2020)

Learning from Differences

Further afield, I have been involved in system change initiatives in Brazil, Hong Kong, Portugal, The Netherlands, Uruguay, and Zambia (Ainscow, 2024a). And in Oman, I worked with Maha Khochen-Bagshaw in developing a guidance document designed to support the promotion of inclusive education across all schools in the country. Its recommendations drew on a review of relevant international literature, as well as evidence collected through our research carried out within the country. These findings were then discussed with a group of representatives from the Ministry of Education, who helped in the formulation of the recommendations.

Particular inspiration comes from Portugal, where the focus on inclusion and equity has led to the overall strengthening of the national education system. Legislation introduced in 2008 led to special schools being transformed into resource centres for inclusion, tasked with supporting their former students, who are now placed in mainstream schools. This pathway continued significantly with the Inclusive Education Act of 2018, which created a further impetus for promoting inclusive education.

Importantly, the Portuguese legislation has moved away from a view that it is necessary to categorise students in order to intervene. Rather, it supports the idea that all children and young people can achieve a profile of competencies and skills at the end of their compulsory education career, even if they follow different learning pathways. It therefore emphasises flexible curricular models, systematic monitoring of the effectiveness of interventions, and an ongoing dialogue between teachers and parents/caregivers (Alves et al., 2020).

Another key feature of the Portuguese education system is the emphasis placed on collaboration. This is facilitated by a well-established pattern of schools working in local clusters – a particular strength in relation to the promotion of inclusive practices and forms of organisation that support the introduction of these ways of working.

In line with current international thinking regarding educational equity and inclusion, as summarised in the previous chapter, the Portuguese legislation emphasises the responsibility of schools to identify barriers to student learning and develop strategies to overcome them. It also calls for a change in school cultures to encourage more multilevel and multidisciplinary interventions, a demonstrated commitment to inclusive practices, and a move away from categorising students.

Since 1995, I have been occasionally involved in these developments in Portugal (Ainscow, 2007, 2024a). Most recently, I was a member of an international team that reviewed progress in the country in relation to inclusion and equity (OECD, 2022). A striking feature of our discussions with stakeholders in different parts of the country was the widespread awareness and acceptance of the principles upon which the national education policies are based. Particularly, impressive was the way that children and young people talked about their pride at being students in a school that is inclusive. Many also talked of the value they gained from being involved with such a diverse range of classmates.

At the same time, there is a noticeable level of awareness at all levels of the Portuguese education system of the dangers associated with using labels in referring to potentially vulnerable groups of students. Frequent mention is also made of the political history of the country that has influenced the concern to see education as a basis for fostering democracy.

A further area of strength in Portugal is the active involvement of community representatives in policy formulation within the school clusters. This includes the appointment of school directors, who are elected for four years. These arrangements provide a basis for engaging community partners to support the promotion of inclusion and equity within a local cluster.

What is most significant, however, is that as the Portuguese education system has moved forward in relation to inclusion over the last two decades, the country has also seen impressive developments in terms of equity. Indeed, it is one of the few countries with a positive trajectory of improvement in all of the subjects assessed by OECD's Programme for International Student Assessment (PISA). In addition, the rate of early leavers from education has reduced significantly, although there are variations between regions.

Drawing Lessons

All of these developments underline my commitment to the importance of context, a theme I return to in the chapters that follow. Keeping this in mind, these experiences led me to formulate a framework for thinking about how to promote inclusion and equity within education systems (see Figure 2.1). Amended from earlier versions (Ainscow, 2005, 2020), this framework emerged from efforts to move education systems in a more inclusive direction. Based on the adage *'the best way to understand an organisation is by trying to change it'*, these

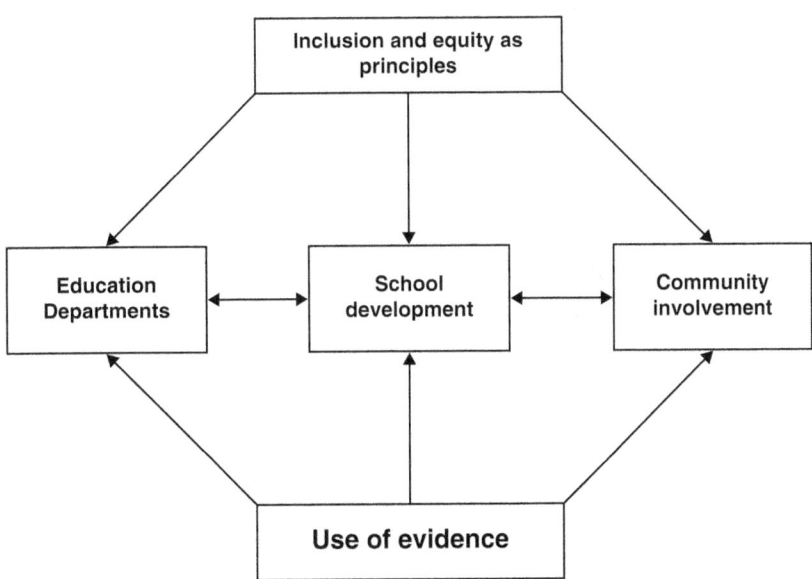

Figure 2.1 A framework for contextual analysis in relation to inclusion and equity

experiences have thrown light on the factors that can facilitate or limit the progress of such initiatives.

As can be seen, the framework places schools at the centre of the analysis. This reinforces the point that moves towards inclusion must be focussed on increasing the capacity of local neighbourhood schools to support the participation and learning of an increasingly diverse range of learners. This is the paradigm shift I have previously described as an 'inclusive turn' (Ainscow, 2007). It argues that moves towards inclusion are about the development of schools, rather than attempts to integrate vulnerable groups of students into existing arrangements.

At the same time, the framework draws attention to a range of contextual factors that bear on the way schools carry out their work. These factors are: the principles that guide policy priorities within an education system; the criteria that are used to evaluate the performance of schools; and the views and actions of others within the local context, including members of the wider community that the schools serve, and the staff of national and local education departments that have responsibility for the coordination of the education system. As I will explain, these are influences that may provide support and encouragement to those in schools who wish to move in an inclusive direction. However, these same factors can also act as obstacles to progress.

In what follows, each of these factors is explained, leading to a series of ideas that need to be considered when analysing a particular context in order to develop future policies. These ideas are guided by a belief that inclusion and equity should not be seen as separate policies. Rather, they should be viewed as principles that inform all policies, particularly those that deal with the curriculum, assessment, supervision, school evaluation, teacher education, and budgets. These principles must also inform all stages of education, from early years provision through to higher education.

Inclusion and Equity as Principles

Terms such as 'equity' and 'inclusion' can be confusing since they may mean different things to different people. This is a particular problem when trying to move forward with others – particularly in schools, where everybody is so busy. Put simply, if there is not a shared understanding of the intended direction of travel, progress will be more difficult. There is, therefore, a need to agree definitions of these concepts.

In establishing a definition for strategic purposes, our earlier research (Ainscow et al., 2006) led us to suggest that inclusion in education should be:

- *Seen as a process.* That is to say, inclusion has to be seen as a never-ending search to find better ways of responding to diversity. It is about learning how to live with differences and learning how to learn from differences. In this way, differences come to be seen more positively as a stimulus for fostering learning, amongst children and adults.
- *Concerned with the identification and removal of barriers.* Consequently, it involves collecting, collating, and evaluating information from a wide variety of sources within particular contexts in order to plan for improvements in policy and practice. It is also about using evidence of various kinds to stimulate creativity and problem-solving.
- *Focused on improving the presence, participation, and achievement of all students.* Here, 'presence' is concerned with where children are educated, and how reliably and punctually they attend; 'participation' relates to the quality of their experiences whilst they are there and, therefore, must incorporate the views of the learners themselves; and 'achievement' is about the outcomes of learning across the curriculum, not merely test or examination results.
- *Involve a particular emphasis on those groups of learners who may be at risk of marginalisation, exclusion, or underachievement.* This indicates the moral responsibility to ensure that those groups that are statistically most at risk are carefully monitored, and that, where necessary, steps are taken to ensure their presence, participation, and achievement within the education system. At the same time, there is a need to keep an eye out for learners who may be overlooked.

My experience is that a well-orchestrated debate about these elements can lead to a wider understanding of the principle of inclusion. Furthermore, such a debate, though by its nature slow and, possibly, never ending, can help to foster the conditions within which schools can feel encouraged to move in a more inclusive direction. Crucially, this must seek to involve all stakeholders, including families, communities, political and religious leaders, and the media. It must also involve those within national and local education district offices. All of which require time and consistent political leadership, as is evident from my account of developments in Portugal.

Inclusive School Development

There is not one single model of what an inclusive school looks like. What is common to highly inclusive schools, however, is that they are welcoming and supportive places for all of their students, not least those with impairments and others who sometimes find learning difficult. This does not prevent these schools from being committed to improving the achievements of all of their students. Indeed, they tend to have a range of strategies for strengthening achievement that are typical of those employed by all effective schools, and the emphasis on supporting vulnerable students does not appear to inhibit these strategies (Dyson, Howes and Roberts, 2004). A key factor is the emphasis placed on tracking and supporting the progress of all students.

The implication is that schools need to be reformed and practices need to be improved in ways that will lead them to respond positively to student diversity – seeing individual differences not as problems to be fixed but as opportunities for enriching learning and facilitating development. Within such a conceptualisation, a consideration of difficulties experienced by students can provide an agenda for change and insights as to how such changes might be brought about. Moreover, this kind of approach is more likely to be successful in contexts where there is a culture of collaboration that encourages and supports problem-solving (Ainscow 2016b; Skrtic, 1991). According to this view, the development of inclusive practices is seen as involving those within a particular context in working together to address barriers to education experienced by some learners

This means that attempts to develop inclusive schools should pay attention to the building of consensus around inclusive values. It implies, too, that school leaders should be selected in the light of their commitment to inclusive values and their capacity to lead in a participatory manner (Riehl, 2000). Finally, the external policy environment should be compatible with inclusive developments in order to support rather than undermine the efforts of schools.

Involving the Wider Community

In order to foster inclusion and equity in education, governments need to mobilise human and financial resources, some of which may not be under their direct control. Forming partnerships among key stakeholders who can support the process of change is therefore essential. These stakeholders include: parents/caregivers; teachers and other education professionals; teacher trainers and researchers; national, local and school-level administrators and managers; policy-makers and service providers in other sectors (e.g., health, child protection, and social services); civic groups in the community; and members of minority groups that are at risk of exclusion.

Family involvement is particularly crucial. In some countries, parents and education authorities already cooperate closely in developing community-based programmes for certain groups of learners, such as those who are excluded because of their gender, social status, or impairments (OECD, 2018). A logical next step is for families to become involved in supporting inclusion in schools.

Where parents lack the confidence and skills to participate in such developments, it may be necessary to engage and build capacity and networks. This could include the creation of family support groups, training parents to work with their children, or building the advocacy skills of parents to negotiate with schools and authorities. Here, it is worth adding that there is evidence that the views of families, including children themselves, can be helpful in bringing new thinking to the efforts of schools to develop more inclusive ways of working (Calderón-Almendros et al., 2020)

This means changing how families and communities work and enriching what they offer to children. In this respect, there are many encouraging examples of what can happen when what schools do is aligned in a coherent strategy with the efforts of other local players – employers, community groups, universities, and public services

(Kerr et al., 2014). This does not necessarily mean schools doing more, but it does imply partnerships beyond the school, where partners multiply the impacts of each other's efforts.

Such developments have implications for the various key stakeholders within education systems. In particular, teachers, especially those in senior positions, have to see themselves as having a wider responsibility for all children, not just those who attend their own schools. They also have to develop patterns of internal organisation that enable them to have the flexibility to cooperate with other schools and with stakeholders beyond the school gate. It means, too, that those who administer education systems have to adjust their priorities and ways of working in response to improvement efforts that are led from within schools.

Education Departments

Policy is made at all levels of an education system, not least at the school and classroom levels (Ainscow, Chapman and Hadfield, 2020). Furthermore, the promotion of equity and inclusion is not simply a technical or organisational change – it is a movement in a clear philosophical direction. Moving to more inclusive ways of working therefore requires changes across an education system. These span from shifts in policy-makers' values and ways of thinking, which enable them to provide a vision shaping a culture of inclusion, to significant changes within schools and the communities they serve.

A culture of inclusion within an education system requires a shared set of assumptions and beliefs among senior staff at the national, district, and school levels that value differences, believe in collaboration, and are committed to offering educational opportunities for all students. However, changing the cultural norms that exist across an education system is difficult to achieve, particularly within contexts that are faced with so many competing pressures and where practitioners tend to work alone in addressing the problems they face. Therefore, leaders at all levels, including those in civil society and other sectors, have to be prepared to analyse their own situations, identify local barriers and facilitators, plan an appropriate development process, and provide support for inclusive practices and effective strategies for monitoring equity in education.

National and district administrators have particularly important roles in promoting inclusive ways of managing schools and education processes. In particular, they need to establish the conditions for challenging non-inclusive, discriminatory educational practices. They also need to build consensus and commitment towards putting the principle of inclusion into practice.

There is also evidence that school-to-school collaboration can strengthen the capacity of individual organisations to respond to learner diversity (Ainscow, 2016b; Muijs et al., 2011). As noted above, collaboration between schools can help to reduce the polarisation of schools, to the particular benefit of those students who are marginalised at the edges of the system. In addition, there is evidence that when schools seek to develop more collaborative ways of working, this can have an impact on how teachers perceive themselves and their work (Rosenholtz, 1989). Specifically, comparisons of practices in different schools can lead teachers to view underachieving students in a new light. In this way, learners who cannot easily be educated within a school's established routines are not seen as 'having problems' but as challenging teachers to re-examine their practices in order to make them more responsive and flexible.

Local coordination is needed in order to encourage this form of area-based collaboration. Here, it is significant that a recent study found that four of the most successful national education systems – Estonia, Finland, Ontario (Canada), and Singapore – all have well-developed systems for coordinating local school districts, regardless of their differing extents of school autonomy or devolution of decision-making (Bubb et al., 2019). In particular, they all have district-level structures that seek to ensure equity as well as excellence.

All of this points to the importance of the ways in which financial resources are allocated within education systems. This can be crucial in creating the flexibility within schools to encourage the sorts of experimentation I have described. Alternatively, it can lead to further segregation, with resources used to provide separate attention for some students – within the school or in separate special schools or classes. In this sense, finance can be a powerful lever for change (Meijer and Watkins, 2019).

Using Evidence

As I have argued, policies for promoting inclusion and equity in education should be based on a clear and widely understood definition of what these terms mean. At the same time, our research suggests that evidence is the life-blood of inclusive development (Ainscow, 2005; Ainscow et al., 2006). Therefore, deciding what kinds of evidence to collect and how to use it requires considerable care, since, within education systems, *what gets measured gets done*. So, for example, many education systems now collect far more statistical data than ever before in order to determine their effectiveness. Most recently this has led to new pressures, as those guiding national policies in many countries have become preoccupied with measuring school outcomes in terms of narrowly defined test scores and comparing their progress with that of other countries through systems such as PISA.

This trend is a double-edged sword precisely because it is such a potent lever for change. On the one hand, data are required in order to monitor the progress of children, evaluate the impact of interventions, review the effectiveness of policies and processes, plan new initiatives, and so on. On the other hand, if effectiveness is evaluated on the basis of narrow, even inappropriate, performance indicators, then the impact can be deeply damaging. Whilst appearing to promote the causes of accountability and transparency, the use of data can, in practice: conceal more than they reveal; invite misinterpretation; and, worse of all, have a perverse effect on the behaviour of professionals. The challenge is, therefore, to harness the potential of evidence as a lever for change, whilst avoiding these potential problems.

England has important lessons to teach us about all of this. Over many years, a combination of test and examination data, plus a national inspection regime, has raised the bar as far as the overall quality of educational provision is concerned. This includes remarkable examples of schools serving highly disadvantaged communities that perform well in respect to the accountability measures. The downside, however, is that these same arrangements have led to a rise in the numbers of students being excluded or placed in separate provisions.

Part of the problem here is that high-stakes accountability systems, such as those that exist in England, tend to focus their school improvement efforts on the most obviously 'failing' schools. This arises not only because of concerns about the impact these schools have on student progress but also because they represent a challenge to the authority and competency of the leaders of school improvement services and the adequacy of local political oversight. The corollary of this focus is that these bureaucratic school improvement systems often define themselves by their ability to 'turn around' failing schools and, in so doing, have little direct engagement with higher-performing schools.

Fullan et al. (2015) argue that accountability is taking responsibility for one's actions and at the core of accountability in educational systems is student learning. In this sense, constantly improving and refining practices so that students can engage in learning tasks is perhaps the single most important responsibility of the teaching profession and educational systems as a whole.

Accountability, as defined in this book, is not limited to mere gains in test scores but on more meaningful learning for all students. Internal accountability occurs when individuals and groups willingly take on personal, professional, and collective responsibility for continuous improvement and success for all students (Hargreaves and Shirley, 2009). External accountability is when system leaders reassure the public through transparency, monitoring, and selective intervention that their system is performing in line with societal expectations and requirements. Therefore, the priority for policymakers should be to create the conditions for internal accountability, because they are more effective in achieving greater overall accountability, including external accountability. In this way, conditions are created that encourage the development of schools that are self-improving.

Self-improving Schools

Efforts in many countries to create schools that can reach all students effectively have often failed to deliver (see, e.g., Giroux and Schmidt, 2004;

OECD, 2010; Schleicher, 2010; Wilkinson and Pickett, 2009). Whilst they may have 'raised the bar', they have not 'closed the gap'. In this book, I present a different way of thinking about this task, one that is mainly led from within schools.

In thinking about what is meant by the idea of self-improving schools I draw on the work of two distinguished scholars, both of who share the same surname. From Andy Hargreaves, I draw on what he and his colleague have described as 'the Fourth Way' (Hargreaves and Shirley, 2009). This is based on what they see as the limitations of three previous ways of thinking about educational change:

- *The First Way* was characterised by state support and professional freedom. In this context, innovation was encouraged and practiced but was often random and inconsistent.
- *The Second Way* attempted to achieve more cohesion and consistency by focusing on market competition and educational standardisation, approaches that were imposed at the expense of professional autonomy.
- *The Third Way* attempted to combine the best of state support and market competition, and balance professional autonomy with accountability. However, it was limited by its emphasis on performance-driven targets and testing.

Reflecting on these earlier formulations, led Hargreaves and Shirley (2020) to conclude:

> Educational standardization has dumbed down our curriculum and burdened our schools with bigger government and overbearing bureaucracy, and has not enabled us to adapt flexibly to the future. These Old Ways of educational change in the 20th century are ill suited to the fast, flexible and vulnerable New World of the 21st century.
>
> (p. x)

As a consequence, they argue that a Fourth Way is now needed. Having analysed examples of school change from various parts of the world that helped them in developing their new formulation, they argue that this:

> ....brings about change through democracy and professionalism, rather than through bureaucracy and market forces. It transfers trust and confidence back from the discredited free market of competition among schools, and reinvests them in the expertise of highly trained and actively trusted professionals. At the same time, it reduces political bureaucracy while energizing public democracy. This means a fundamental shift in teachers' professionalism that restores greater autonomy from government and introduces more openness to and engagement with parents and communities. The Fourth Way, therefore, means significant change for everyone – governments, parents, and teacher unions alike.
>
> (p. 72)

Within the Fourth Way, teachers set shared targets, rather than attempting to meet the targets demanded by others. In this way, it is argued, democracy plus professionalism replaces bureaucracy and the market – it is about less government and more about democracy. Within the Fourth Way, the government is not there to drive and deliver but to steer and support. Finally, in the Fourth Way, responsibility comes before accountability, because it is collective responsibility for performance that ultimately will lift the system. As a result:

> The Fourth Way pushes beyond standardization, data-driven decision making, and target-obsessed distractions to forge an equal and interactive partnership between the people, the profession, and their government. It enables educational leaders to "let go" of the details of change, steering broadly whenever they can and intervening directly only when they must - to restore safety, avoid harm and remove incompetence and corruption from the system.
>
> (Hargreaves and Shirley, 2009, p. 71)

Whilst not suggesting that the projects that have informed the arguments presented in this book were driven directly by these ideas, my analysis of the lessons that can be learnt from what happened most certainly was. In particular, my conclusion as to what is needed to foster the development of self-improving schools is based on the argument that we need to go *'beyond standardization, data-driven decision making, and target-obsessed distractions to forge an equal and interactive partnership between the people, the profession, and their government'*.

Related to this, my argument also makes extensive use of David Hargreaves's ground-breaking conceptualization of what a self-improving system would look like. In a series of what he describes as 'think pieces', written for the National College for School Leadership in England, Hargreaves sets out a set of important ideas that are crucial to the suggestions I make in this book (Hargreaves, 2010, 2011, 2012).

In the first of his think pieces, Hargreaves argues that there are four 'building blocks' for the development of a self-improving system: capitalising on the benefits of clusters of schools; adopting a local solutions approach; stimulating co-construction between schools; and expanding the concept of system leadership. He further suggests that in order to move forward these building blocks have to be strengthened, so that schools collaborate in more effective forms of professional development and school improvement. These important themes are explored further in subsequent chapters.

Conclusion

Where inclusion and equity are seen as discrete policies, they are likely to become someone's job. In contrast, I suggest that the aim must be to make them everyone's responsibility. This points to the first of my propositions: **inclusion and equity should be seen as principles that inform all policies,** not least those that are concerned with the curriculum, assessment processes, teacher education, accountability and funding. At the same time, evidence of various kinds is seen as a major driver for educational reforms.

As I have argued in this chapter, the starting point for making decisions about the evidence to collect at the system level should be with agreed definitions of inclusion and equity. In other words, we must *measure what we value*, rather than is often the case, valuing what we can more easily measure. This means that evidence collected within an education system needs to relate to the *'presence, participation and achievement'* of all students, with an emphasis placed on those groups of learners regarded to be 'at risk of marginalisation, exclusion or underachievement'. In this respect, as argued by Hopkins (2024), the achievement and learning of students is a moral purpose that should be central to what schools and teachers do.

Notes

1 https://www.eenet.org.uk/resources/docs/Index%20English.pdf
2 https://www.ibe.unesco.org/en/node/103?hub=41

3
CHANGING EDUCATION SYSTEMS

Equity is a major concern within the four national education systems of the United Kingdom, each of which has a discreet education policy. For the purposes of the arguments I present in this chapter, the English context serves as an advanced example of an internationally widespread direction of travel, i.e. a competitive and fragmented school system, operating in a highly unequal society, in which wider state support systems are increasingly being rolled back; and where inequalities are growing and more children are living in poverty. At the same time, schools serving the poorest contexts and student populations are often the most vulnerable. In addition, wider support for children and families, which could help to mitigate the impacts of inequities arising from home and community circumstances, has also been greatly reduced and fragmented.

Together, these factors have led to growing inequalities within the English education, since low outcomes are concentrated in the poorest areas and the schools serving them. These inequalities were growing pre-pandemic and there is evidence to suggest they have accelerated since (Kerr and Ainscow, 2022).

The last 20 years have seen efforts to address this issue through a series of 'challenge' programmes, the first of which took place in London. In what follows I examine the evidence regarding what has been called the 'London effect', before going on to focus on the work of follow-up challenge programmes, first in Greater Manchester and later in Wales.

My involvement in these projects was as an adviser, using knowledge from relevant research to guide decision-making. This provided privileged access to information about the way decisions are made within an education system, from the levels of government ministers, senior civil servants, school leaders, and classroom teachers. It also provided frequent reminders of the cultural, social, and political complexities involved when trying to bring about changes in the way that an education system does its business.

London Challenge

The London Challenge was introduced during a period of successive Labour Governments (1997–2010) as part of an intensification of political interest in the standard and management of education. This led to a series of centralised national strategies to strengthen practices of teaching and leadership. At the same time, competition between schools was increasingly seen to be one of the keys to 'driving up standards', whilst further reducing the control of local authorities over provision. All of this was intended to 'liberate' schools from the bureaucracy of local government and establish a form of market place. In this way, it was argued, families would have greater choice as to which school their children would attend, informed by school reports from the national inspection agency, Ofsted, and the annual publication of school test and examination results.

During that period, there was also a number of policy efforts to address factors which lie beyond schools. These recognised that children's progress cannot be divorced from other aspects of their development and what happens to them outside school – in their families, neighbourhoods, and more widely. These initiatives sought to improve and equalise educational outcomes, by aligning schools' core business of teaching and learning with interventions targeting other aspects of children's lives. All of this was part of a Children's Plan which set out a framework for organising child and family services based on the principle that 'Every Child Matters', i.e. that all children should be healthy, stay safe, enjoy and achieve, make a positive contribution and achieve economic well-being.

London Challenge was a further element in this reform programme. It began in 2003, concentrating on the improvement of secondary schools. By 2007, the national inspection agency, Ofsted, was reporting that standards in these schools had improved 'dramatically' and that the city had recorded its best-ever examination results, with its state secondary school students leading the rest of the country for a third year running (Ainscow, 2015). During the later stages of the initiative, I became involved as a participant-observer as I prepared for the role I was to take on later in Greater Manchester.

Analysing the Impact

As a result of their research into the success of London Challenge, Kidson and Norris (2014) conclude that it was a distinctive example of public service improvement that was practitioner-focused, highly collaborative, and applied across a system. They note, too, that all the people they interviewed felt that the initiative had made a major contribution to the exceptional improvement in the capital's schools. This was attributed to: the way credible professionals supported their peers; the powerful sense of moral purpose and positive framing; and the close working relationships of officials, advisers, and ministers, which was focused on a shared, data-led view of where there were strengths and weaknesses in the schools.

There are, however, a range of other views about what made the difference in London. For example, Lowe (2015) points out that other government interventions taking place around the same time may also have had an impact. He mentions Teach First, a graduate recruitment scheme launched in 2002 to coax top young graduates into the classroom, which was widely used in London. He also notes the possible impact of the national inspection agency, Ofsted, and new transparency in relation to school results. In addition, Lowe argues that the role of primary schools cannot be ignored, noting that the national strategies in literacy and numeracy were perhaps taken up far more enthusiastically in London than elsewhere. Meanwhile, Burgess (2014) introduces another perspective, suggesting that the basis for London's progress was the ethnic composition of its school population. It is worth noting, too, that there is a view that London schools have benefited from preferential financing.

A further worrying factor that should not be overlooked is subsequent reports that London schools have seen increases in both temporary and permanent exclusion rates.[1] This reminds me of a comment made by a key figure involved in London Challenge who referred to how they had learnt to 'pull some tricks' in order to improve examination results. All of which underlines the complexities involved in system change and the problems that exist when trying to establish the nature of the 'local causality' at play within it (Hadfield and Jopling, 2018).

In the light of this success, in 2008 the government extended the London programme for a further three years and expanded it to primary schools. At the same time, the creation of a generic City Challenge programme was announced that would include two other regions, the Black Country, in the West Midlands, and Greater Manchester. This led me to experience yet another intensive period of rethinking.

The Greater Manchester Challenge

In 2007, I was appointed as the government's Chief Adviser for the Greater Manchester Challenge, a three-year initiative involving over 1,100 schools in ten local authorities, with a government investment of around £50 million (see Ainscow, 2015, for a detailed account of this initiative). The decision to invest this large amount reflected a concern regarding educational standards in the city region, particularly amongst children and young people from disadvantaged backgrounds. It is important to note that both the London and Greater Manchester Challenge programmes each had the active involvement of a Government Minister. In terms of the impact, the presence of high-status political leadership should not be overlooked.

A detailed analysis of the context led to the conclusion that plenty of good practice existed within Greater Manchester schools. Consequently, it was decided that collaboration and networking between schools of the sort that had occurred in London would be key strategies for strengthening the overall capacity of the system to reach out to vulnerable groups of learners. More specifically this involved a series of inter-connected activities for 'moving knowledge around' in order to build a self-improving school system (Ainscow, 2012, 2015).

With this in mind, Families of Schools were set up. This approach partnered ten or so schools that serve similar populations whilst, at the same time, encouraging partnerships amongst schools that were not in direct competition with one another because they did not serve the same neighbourhoods. Led by headteachers, the Families of Schools proved to be successful in strengthening collaborative processes within the city region, although the impact was varied.

In terms of schools working in the most disadvantaged contexts, more intensive school partnerships were found to be the most powerful means of fostering improvements (Hutchings et al., 2012). Most notably, the Keys to Success programme led to striking improvements in the performance of some 200 Greater Manchester schools facing the most challenging circumstances. A common feature of almost all of these interventions was that progress was achieved through carefully matched pairings (or, sometimes, trios) of schools that, once again, cut across social 'boundaries' of various kinds, including those that separate schools that are in different local authorities (Ainscow, 2013). In this way, expertise that was previously trapped in particular contexts became more widely available.

Whilst increased collaboration of this sort proved to be vital as a strategy for developing more effective ways of working, the experience of Greater Manchester shows that it was not enough. The essential additional ingredient was an engagement with evidence that can bring an element of mutual challenge to such collaborative processes. We found that evidence was at its most powerful where partner schools are carefully matched and know what they are trying to achieve. Evidence also helped schools go beyond cosy relationships that may have little or no impact on outcomes. As the headteacher who led one effective partnership commented: *'If you don't have the data on the table you are just being nice to one another'*. Consequently, schools need to base their relationships on evidence about each other's strengths and weaknesses, so that they can challenge each other to improve.

Another effective strategy to facilitate the movement of expertise was the creation of various types of hub schools. For example, some of the hubs provided support for other schools about ways to engage students with English as an additional language. Similarly, so-called 'teaching schools'[2] providing professional development programmes focused on bringing about improvements in classroom practice.

A key factor in the success of both the London and Greater Manchester Challenge programmes was the involvement of teams of expert advisers. Chosen because of their track records of leading successful school improvement, they were given the mandate and resources to intervene in schools, helping them to develop, implement, and monitor the impact of their own improvement plans (I explain more about their work in Chapter 7).

We also found it useful to introduce easy-to-recall formulations that could help busy colleagues to articulate to one other a sense of common purpose. So, for example, in an attempt to create the sense of a common purpose, it was agreed that the focus of the Greater Manchester Challenge activities would be on 'three As'. These were that all children and young people: should have high *Aspirations* for their learning and life chances; are ensured *Access* to high-quality educational experiences; and *Achieve* the highest possible standards in learning. These terms were then incorporated into the Challenge logo.

The emphasis on collaboration and experimentation was further signalled by other carefully chosen language used to talk about the Challenge, formally and informally, at meetings and through an occasional newsletter sent out to schools. For example, frequent mention was made of the importance of *'moving knowledge around'*, recognising that *'most of the expertise that is needed is here in Greater Manchester'*, and *'getting behind those in schools who can make things happen'*. I also reminded people that *'this is not about doing more of the same'*, encouraging people to understand that we did have a degree of freedom to experiment, albeit within a context where we were all under pressure *'to deliver'*.

Evaluation

An independent evaluation of the City Challenge programme concluded that it had been largely successful in achieving its objectives

(Hutchings et al., 2012). Commenting on this, the authors of the report argue:

> Clearly a great many factors contributed to these improvements, including national policies and strategies and the considerable efforts of headteachers and staff. However, these factors apply everywhere in the country. The most plausible explanation for the greater improvement in Challenge areas is that the City Challenge programme was responsible. The vast majority of stakeholders at all levels who contributed to this evaluation attributed the additional improvements that have been made in these areas to the work of City Challenge.
>
> (p. vi)

The evaluators also concluded that the strategic factors contributing to its success were: the timescale; the focus on specific urban areas; flexibility of approach; use of expert advisers and bespoke solutions; school staff learning from practice in other schools; and the programme ethos of trust, support, and encouragement. Looking to implications for other contexts, I would add that the involvement of headteachers acting as system leaders became an important factor. As I go on to explain, this was a lesson that informed developments in other contexts.

A National Initiative in Wales

In 2014, I was invited by the Welsh Government to lead Schools Challenge Cymru, a national initiative to promote equity across the country, the design of which was much influenced by what had happened in City Challenge. Wales shares a close political and social history with the rest of Great Britain, and almost everyone speaks English. However, the country has retained a distinct cultural identity and is officially bilingual, with Welsh being spoken by about 20% of the population, mostly in the north and west of the country. Although it is part of the United Kingdom, Wales has a form of self-government created in 1998 following a referendum and has its own education policies. There are 22 local authorities responsible for a range of public services, including education.

The purpose of Schools Challenge Cymru was to accelerate progress across the education system. In particular, it aimed to bring about rapid improvements in the performance of schools serving the more disadvantaged communities and use lessons from these developments to strengthen the capacity of the education system to improve itself. The budget was approximately 20 million pounds per year.

Building on the earlier experiences in London and Greater Manchester, the Welsh initiative worked with 40 secondary schools serving disadvantaged communities (designated as the *'Pathways to Success'*) and their local primary school partners. Similar to City Challenge, a team of expert advisers was involved in supporting these schools.

The challenge advisers were directly accountable to the Minister for Education and Skills. As was the case in City Challenge, the Minister was closely associated with the initiative, visiting each of the schools at least twice over the first 18 months. This provided the political mandate that Claeys et al. (2014) argue is essential to improvement strategies that mainly emphasise bottom-up action.

The results showed that overall attainment in examinations taken by almost all students at the age of 16, across the Pathways to Success schools, improved by seven percentage points, with 87% of the schools securing improvements in this measure. This rate of improvement was faster than the overall progress made across Wales over the same period. The attainment of students entitled to free school meals[3] across the schools improved by 8.2 percentage points, with 74% of the schools securing improvements.

In making sense of these trends, it is important to remember that the participating schools were chosen because of the particular challenges they faced and the fact that they had, to varying degrees, performed poorly over many years. Indeed, in a few cases, the conditions in the schools were amongst the worst I have experienced in my career. Nevertheless, some of them became striking examples of what is possible when the expertise and energy within schools are mobilised. However, these gains were hard won and were likely to remain fragile without continuing support.

Beyond the 40 schools, there was evidence that Schools Challenge Cymru began to have a ripple effect across the education system in ways that raised expectations about how rapidly improvements can be achieved (Hadfield and Ainscow, 2018). This has implications for efforts to improve outcomes for learners from low-income families, where low expectations can be a factor in preventing their progress (Kerr and West, 2010).

An independent evaluation of Schools Challenge Cymru concluded that the quality of leadership and management had improved in the majority of Pathways to Success schools (Carr, Brown and Morris, 2017). In two-fifths of the schools, involvement in the programme was considered to be largely, or wholly, responsible for the changes in student engagement. Some schools were optimistic, too, about sustaining perceived improvements in attendance, hoping that good attendance would become the norm. The report also concluded that the programme had strengthened professional development within the schools and, in some cases, extended it.

A Regional Challenge

A further relevant example of a system-wide change strategy took place in the Central South Wales (CSW) region, an initiative that overlapped with the Schools Challenge Cymru programme (Hadfield and Ainscow, 2018).

The CSW Challenge was instigated by the Directors of Education of the five authorities in the region, one of which is the capital city, Cardiff, and received endorsement from local politicians. At the same time, staff of the existing regional consortium played important roles in supporting its programme of activities. Additional funding and support was provided through Schools Challenge Cymru as part of its capacity-building role across the country.

Developed in consultation with representatives of schools in the region, the overall purpose was to transform educational outcomes by improving leadership and teaching, and by finding ways of reducing the impact of poverty on educational outcomes. This was to be achieved, it was argued, by building the capacity of schools to be self-improving. Reference was also made to the development of a culture that embraces innovation, and enables teachers and leaders to work together to improve practice in ways that are informed by research and have a positive impact on students' achievement and progress.

Reflecting much of the thinking of City Challenge in England, the CSW strategy was intended to be *'by schools, for schools'*. With this as a guiding principle, activities were planned and coordinated by a strategy group made up of headteachers.

At a conference for over 400 headteachers that launched the CSW Challenge in February 2014, I talked about lessons that could be learnt from research and experiences elsewhere, particularly City Challenge in England. At the end of the morning, many of the participants expressed their enthusiasm for the rationale presented and the proposed strategies outlined by members of the strategy group. However, a few commented that they had met in the same conference centre on a number of earlier occasions to hear about what seemed like equally impressive plans. Apparently, none of these had led to significant change.

As if that was insufficient as a source of anxiety, the education reporter of a leading national newspaper wrote about what seemed to him to have been a successful conference. However, in commenting on the suggestion that schools would be expected to cooperate across the borders of the five partner local authorities, he wrote that the *'desire to blur the boundaries between schools – as well as bordering local authorities – may be wishful thinking. Breaking down age-old barriers between schools of different hues will be no mean feat and it will be interesting to see whether or not headteachers are willing to play ball'*. The encouraging news is that over the following four years, many heads were willing to play ball, despite the many obstacles they faced.

The Rationale

The ideas that underpinned the CSW Challenge were as follows:

- Schools as communities where collaborative enquiry is used to improve practice;
- Groupings of schools engaging in joint practice development;
- Where necessary, more intensive partnerships supporting schools facing difficulties;

- Families and Community organisations supporting the work of schools;
- Coordination of the system provided by school leaders; and
- Local authorities working together to act as the 'conscience of the system'.

As can be seen, this placed the responsibility for the co-ordination of the system on the shoulders of school leaders, with local authorities holding them to account.

The espoused aim of having current school leaders co-ordinate the new collaborative system was enacted in practice by the creation of the strategy group, consisting of headteachers drawn from each of the authorities and all phases of the system. The group itself was not an operational decision-making forum; rather, it set the overall direction of the Challenge. Partnered with staff from the regional consortium, these heads were seconded from local schools and became directly involved in leading collaborative working and the setting up of new structures.

At the inception of the CSW Challenge in 2014, overall student performance in the region was below the national average. Three years later, this had improved, so that in key stage 4 (students aged 14-16) their performance in national tests (i.e. GCSE examinations) was above the national average at the 'Level 2 threshold' (achieved when they gained 5 A*s to C grade qualifications).

This overall trend was driven by improvements in all five authorities, with the two most underperforming improving to the greatest extent and the other three performing above the national average. At the same time, there were encouraging trends in relation to the average progress of students eligible for free school meals (an indicator of social deprivation) and other students. These positive trends in attainment were matched by similar trends in the reduction of the numbers of schools categorised as requiring additional support as part of national accountability arrangements.

Barriers to Progress

Common features of all the system reform initiatives described in this chapter were an emphasis on bottom-up leadership within a context of top-down political mandate, and the use of evidence to inform design and implementation. However, we found that the adoption of this thinking was sometimes difficult because of a series of interconnected barriers. Broadly stated, these relate to:

- *Social factors*, including the extent to which relationships exist that encourage the sharing of expertise through mutual support and challenge;
- *Political factors*, due to the impact of the attitudes and preferences of key partners; and
- *Cultural factors*, created by local traditions and the expectations of those involved as to what is possible.

In what follows I reflect on my involvement in the Challenge projects, plus more recent experiences of the Scottish Attainment Challenge and other smaller place-based developments in England, in order to make sense of these barriers (see Ainscow, Chapman and Hadfield, 2020, for accounts of these initiatives).

Social Factors

In reflecting further on these experiences, it does seem that 'size matters'. To give a striking example, I contributed to planning in a small rural district, where there were concerns about poor standards in the schools. To an outsider with lots of urban experience, the closeness of the links between headteachers in this community seemed to be a positive feature in terms of the encouragement of greater collaboration.

In line with the thinking developed in this book, I encouraged a restructuring that would enable existing good practices within local schools to be made available to more students and encourage joint practice developments. This was to be achieved through the strengthening of various forms of cooperation between the schools. It required new roles for headteachers, some of who volunteered to take on the task of leading these developments. With this in mind, I consulted with all the heads within the authority. As a result, a new momentum for change quickly emerged in the primary sector, where a group of five relatively successful headteachers took on responsibility for moving things forward.

In discussing their roles, these heads commented on the social complexities they faced in getting colleagues to cooperate. In particular, they commented on the implications of the fact that amongst schools in a small community *'everybody knows one another'*. They explained that relationships were usually warm and cordial, something that I certainly experienced. However, it was also apparent that this closeness between colleagues had the potential to create subtle barriers to genuine collaboration between schools. One headteacher summed this when she said, *'we don't bare our souls around here'*. In other words, if you have a problem in your school, you keep it to yourself. Clearly, such a social climate can make it difficult for colleagues to support one another. It also means that the external researcher – there to support and advise – faces what may well be hidden barriers to an understanding of the dynamics of the local school system.

It follows that the involvement of an 'outsider', acting in the role of adviser, requires constructive relationships with key partners. I have found that maintaining such relationships creates many dilemmas that usually have to be addressed when and where they occur. For example, a meeting was held with senior officers in one local authority where civil servants and I were concerned about the poor quality of support provided for primary schools. At times the meeting became heated, as authority staff attempted to challenge our analysis. One colleague, in particular, was clearly distressed. Indeed, at one point he explained that he had never felt so personally humiliated during his long professional career. This particular meeting did not lead to an immediate outcome that could be described as being positive. Nevertheless, I felt that it was necessary to intervene in a context where thinking and practices were limiting opportunities for children. Subsequently, a series of further meetings did lead to agreement as to necessary actions to strengthen the work of this particular local authority in supporting its schools.

In reflecting on incidents such as this one, I am occasionally reminded of Robert Bales' theory of group systems that we had used in earlier research (see Ainscow, Hargreaves and Hopkins, 1995). As Bales predicts, attempts to get different stakeholders to pull together lead to tensions between the need to establish cohesion amongst groups and taking actions to achieve our goals. Put simply, it is relatively easy to maintain cooperation until the moments when hard decisions had to be made, most particularly regarding the setting of priorities and the allocation of resources.

Political Factors

The most striking evidence of the political nature of large-scale system change projects occurred following two national elections. This led to new ministers being appointed and, as a result, the Challenge projects losing much of their political mandate. The projects did continue, however, although with less power to make things happen. Having said that, in the case of one of the initiatives, we have evidence of the continuing impact of its legacy six years later, most strikingly in terms of partnerships and networks (Armstrong and Ainscow, 2018). This reminds us that time-limited developments that seem not to have had longer impact can often have overlooked legacies.

The initiatives I have described took place during an unprecedented period of change within their education systems, not least in terms of decision-making regarding education policy. The ways in which decisions were made regarding changes varied across the countries. England was in the process of giving schools much greater autonomy, especially in the use of financial resources and the appointment of staff members. This also led to a much greater role for headteachers as system leaders, working together to coordinate collaborative improvement efforts.

In all of the contexts, the role of the local authority in the management of the school system was being questioned and, in the case of England, massively reduced (Salokangas and Ainscow, 2017). Meanwhile, Wales and Scotland continued in a much more centralised way, with decisions mainly shared between the national government and local authorities. As a result, in both these countries, there are continuing tensions between the two levels regarding policies, the determination of priorities, and the use of resources (Ainscow, 2023b).

During the setting up phases of the Challenge programmes, much use was made by government officials of the term 'partnership' in describing what was to happen. I sensed that for some local authority colleagues this was a source of irritation, in that the decisions to have the initiatives were largely imposed by national governments as processes of intervention in areas of concern.

One factor behind these tensions was different views as to what needed to happen in order to improve education systems: put bluntly, a difference between those who believe in locally led development and others who continue to adopt a centralising perspective. For example, the latter view was starkly expressed in an email sent to colleagues within the DfES in London during the City Challenge period, which stated that, as far as improving attainment amongst disadvantaged students was concerned, 'the strategy must be exactly the same, whether it is in Plymouth (*in the south west of England*), or in Sunderland (*in the far north east*)'. The implication being, we know what to do: it just needs to be done, irrespective of context.

This instinct to direct from the centre occasionally surfaced at meetings of the challenge advisers, when civil servant colleagues took opportunities to brief the groups on the latest proposals from central government and the necessity for reporting back to central government through complex mechanisms. In general, the teams found these inputs helpful in that they made them feel ahead of the game regarding policy decisions, although the bureaucratic reporting and accountability systems were perceived to be frustrating and heavy handed. In these cases, my concern was that, too often, the meetings gave the wrong message in respect to the overall theory of change we had adopted.

A striking example of this, that created a significant distraction, was as a result of the publication of a White Paper about the reform of the English education system. The civil servant who led on this initiative as far as primary schools were concerned became particularly dogged in her efforts to impose a centrally determined strategy on the schools. With this in mind, for some months she guided the agenda of the team of primary school advisers in a direction that represented a significant deviation from the rationale we had developed together.

During this phase, my own involvement in decision-making was clearly marginalised.

Sustainability was a major concern in all of the initiatives. The history of large-scale, heavily funded improvement projects is that, even when they are seen to be initially successful, the impact gradually fades once the additional resources are taken away (Ainscow, 2015). One way of addressing this problem is to strengthen the so-called middle tier, the administrative arrangements that are intended to coordinate the development of education provision within a local area. In Wales, for example, this meant the 22 local authorities, which are grouped together in four regional consortia that are intended to support school improvement efforts. There are, however, potential barriers to making such regional partnerships work, including the large geographical areas that they sometimes cover, competing philosophies and educational agendas, and the struggles they can create regarding decision-making across political boundaries. I return to this theme in later chapters

Within national systems that continue to emphasise top-down accountability, the responses of local authorities can also, at times, act as a barrier to school-level innovation. For example, one very experienced head teacher, appointed to improve a school in difficulty, talked about local authority officers frequently commenting negatively regarding the ways he dealt with minor administrative matters.

Cultural Factors

Efforts to inject greater pace into the improvement of schools within the Challenge programmes drew attention to the untapped potential that exists within schools. They also threw light on the factors that had limited the impact of earlier improvement efforts. Our monitoring suggested that these barriers mainly relate to existing ways of working, which, although well intended, consume time and resources, and delay action in the field. A head teacher in Wales echoed the views of many others when he commented that, in his part of the world, school improvement is like trying to drive more quickly down a road with speed bumps every few yards.

The experience of the various initiatives described in this chapter suggests that many of the 'bumps' relate to existing ways of working, which reflect taken-for-granted assumptions as to what is possible. Although well intended, these traditions often consume time and resources and delay action. They include, for example, the over emphasis placed by some local authorities on putting schools, particularly those facing challenging circumstances, under unnecessary pressure. This tends to demoralise the key agents of change, i.e. the staff in the schools. It can also lead to considerable time being wasted on debating and disputing plans and targets. My experience is that, whilst these approaches can be helpful, without powerful support strategies they are unlikely to lead to sustainable change.

Linked to this were actions by some local authority staff that limited the freedom of school leaders to take responsibility for their own improvement. In particular, we found that there were often multiple reporting arrangements, leading school leaders to spend much time preparing reports for different audiences, attending various review and scrutiny meetings, and being given different (and at times conflicting) advice on the improvements required and how they can be achieved. Despite calls for the empowerment of schools and headteachers, this limited freedom can foster a sense of dependency on outsiders to lead improvement efforts, rather than empowering those in schools to take responsibility and be accountable for improved outcomes. In such situations, school leaders can feel undermined and disenfranchised. As a result, they tend to make poor decisions, and therefore find it more difficult to prioritise their improvement strategies.

In addressing these barriers, efforts are needed to clarify the roles of local authorities. Specifically, this requires local authority staff to know, trust, and support school personnel, and provide appropriate encouragement to improve. These changes in roles and responsibilities are particularly challenging during periods of transition, as locally led improvement strategies are developing, but they are precursors to achieving rapid progress.

There are also barriers related to the uncertainly that exists within governments about how to support the development of locally driven collaborative improvement. One step to reduce that uncertainty is to recognise that using the power of collaboration as a means of achieving equity in schools requires an approach to national policy implementation that fosters greater flexibility at the local level and gives practitioners the space to analyse their particular circumstances and determine priorities accordingly.

What Works

The approaches to system change that I have presented involve processes of social learning: the bringing together of different types of expertise to address challenges faced in particular contexts. This approach is contrary to the *'what works'* approach to educational change that is becoming dominant in an increasing number of countries (Biesta, 2010). This approach is based on very different assumptions regarding how to use research knowledge to inform improvement efforts. It assumes that the task of researchers is to convince practitioners to change their behaviour in light of evidence from elsewhere. The implication is that teachers are there to 'deliver' practices that have been designed and evaluated by researchers – this means that practitioners are constructed as users of expert knowledge, not as knowledge creators.

In an earlier era, this approach involved systematic reviews of research findings that were expected to facilitate evidence-based policy-making and practice. Institutional moves were made to increase the production of such reviews; for example, the Evidence for Policy and Practice Information Coordinating Centre was established at the Institute for Education, University of London. Hammersley (2001) expresses concerns about the rather instrumental model these reviews present of the relationship between research and practice. Furthermore, he argues, it involves a search for technical solutions to what may well be political or social problems.

I contend that it is not proven that providing solutions to practical problems, or evaluating them, is the most important contribution that research can make to policy-making and practice. Furthermore, the what works movement adopts a view of the role of educational research which can undermine practitioners' expertise because it privileges certain kinds of research evidence. In contrast, I am arguing for the use of collaborative inquiry-based approaches, which might well incorporate evidence from academic research, to address the technical, cultural, and political aspects of change.

Conclusion

The evidence from the system change projects described in this chapter suggests that schools are willing to support one another, even within policy contexts where competition is a major policy driver for improvement. However, this is difficult to achieve and often remains fragile as a result of policy contradictions that pull stakeholders in a different direction.

More recently, this has become even more difficult within the context of England as a result of an increased emphasis on school autonomy, competition, and choice. In this particular policy context, it became clear that some form of locally led coordination is needed in order to determine relevant areas for development, engage stakeholders, and broker partnerships (Ainscow et al., 2023). The successful examples of this that we have found suggest a possible way forward. They involve shared leadership from within schools, built on previous experience of schools collaborating that had helped to develop relationships and confidence in sharing responsibility. I return to this theme in later chapters.

The accounts also point to the importance of having a political mandate for system reform efforts. As I have explained, such mandates are usually temporary, not least because of political processes that create timescales for policies and, indeed, for political appointments. The implication is that progress usually remains fragile.

Together, these experiences lead to the second of my propositions for system reform in relation to inclusion and equity: *barriers to the presence, participation and achievement of learners should be identified and addressed*. In particular, progress requires a move away from explanations of educational failure that focus on the characteristics of individual children and their families, towards an analysis of contextual factors that impact on the experiences of learners within schools.

Notes

1 https://www.london.gov.uk/press-releases/assembly/the-link-between-school-exclusions-violent-crime
2 The idea of teaching schools, which act as professional development hubs, subsequently became part of national policy in England.
3 An indication of economic disadvantage.

4
Inquiring Schools

Policy is made at all levels of an education system, particularly at the classroom level. Indeed, as far as students are concerned, teachers are policy-makers. The implication is that attempts to bring about system change must involve them. Their thinking and actions are what matter most as far as inclusion and equity is concerned.

In this chapter, I explore how inclusive practices can be developed, the forms of school organisation that are required to support such efforts, and the implications for leadership practices. I argue that successful change is more likely in contexts where there is a culture of collaboration that encourages and supports problem-solving. According to this view, the development of inclusive practices is seen as involving those within a particular context in working together to address barriers to education experienced by some learners.

At the same time, I argue that the way forward in relation to educational reform is to learn from such experiences. In this respect I am inspired by the work of Richard Elmore (2004) who concludes: '... *the life of schools and classrooms have much to teach policymakers about the design and implementation of good policy. To succeed, school reform has to happen "from the inside out"'* (p. 3)

Teacher Development

Central to the argument I present in this chapter is a need to create the conditions within which teachers are involved in processes of evidence-based professional learning within their schools. With this focus in mind, I begin by drawing on some of the findings of our earlier review of relevant international research (see Messiou and Ainscow, 2016)

According to Opfer and Pedder (2010), teacher professional development relies heavily on supportive interactions amongst staff members at all levels of a school in order for the process to be effective. They also indicate that the term 'development' signposts that this is intended to lead to changes in practice and, therefore, increased effectiveness: the implication being that successful teacher development is largely dependent on what practitioners perceive effectiveness to be. This means that much of teacher development must occur within schools and, in particular, within classrooms. In this way, there is a direct focus on the concerns of individual teachers and their workplace contexts.

All of this demands organisational flexibility within schools and the active support of senior staff who are prepared to encourage and support processes of experimentation (Leithwood and Reihl, 2003). Where this is focused on issues related to learner diversity, it is also likely to involve challenges to the thinking of those within a particular organisation (West, Ainscow and Nottman, 2003).

Locating professional development within schools and classrooms is a way of making better use of the expertise that already exists (Ainscow et al., 2012b). It also relates to what is known about how practices develop within the workplace. Significant here is the influential thinking of Etienne Wenger (1998), who explains how practice develops through processes of social learning within particular contexts. In so doing, he provides a framework that can be used to analyse learning in social contexts such as schools. At the centre of this framework is the concept of a 'community of practice', a social group engaged in the sustained pursuit of a shared enterprise within a particular context. I return to the potential importance of this formulation later in the chapter.

Collaboration

As a result of a review of publications about teacher professional development, Avalos (2011) highlights the importance of collaboration as a facilitator for learning amongst teachers, in particular for changing or reinforcing teaching practices. There is also an assumption that practitioners have to take greater responsibility for their own professional learning. So, for example, Hayes (2000) suggests that effective teacher development can be promoted if and when used in line with collaborative and context-specific involvement of teachers, who have ownership over their personal development.

The importance of collaboration in professional development is also highlighted by a series of research syntheses from the Centre for Evidence-Informed Policy and Practice in Education. In particular, one of its reviews concludes that collaboration between teachers, coupled with active experimentation, may be more effective in changing practice than reflection and discussion about practice alone (Cordingley et al., 2005). In addition, Hill, Beisiegel and Jacob (2013) argue: *'Through studies conducted over the past two decades, scholars have identified programme design elements thought to maximize teacher learning, including a strong content focus, inquiry-oriented learning approaches, collaborative participation, and coherence with school curricula and policies'* (p. 476).

Collaborative participation is, therefore, an essential factor in maximising teacher professional learning. This explains the recent emphasis on the use of forms of collaborative inquiry to facilitate teacher development within studies carried out in a variety of contexts, such as Canada, Europe, and the United States (e.g., Bleicher, 2014; Butler and Schnellert, 2012; Cain and Milovic, 2010; Horn & Little, 2010; Jaipal & Figg, 2011; Vaino, Holbrook and Rannikmae, 2013). It also points to the possibility of 'joint practice development', which Fielding et al. (2005) define as learning new ways of working through mutual engagement that opens up and shares practices with others. Joint practice development, they suggest, involves: interaction and mutual development related to practice; recognises that each partner in the interaction has something to offer; and is research-informed, often involving collaborative inquiry. Through such activities, teachers develop ways of talking that enable them to articulate details about their practices. In this way, they are able to share ideas about their ways of working with colleagues. This also assists individuals to reflect on their own ways of working, as well as the thinking behind their actions.

It is important to bear in mind, however, that such sharing of ideas is far from easy in the context of schools, partly because of the intensity of the day but also because of the nature of teacher knowledge. Commenting on this, David Hargreaves (2003) draws attention to how much of teachers' knowledge is tacit and therefore difficult to articulate. He argues that this is the main reason why it has proved so difficult to transfer good practice from one teacher to another. This leads him to conclude that what he describes as 'social capital' is needed within teaching communities. Here, social capital represents shared values and assumptions that, because they are commonly 'owned' by community members, are available for all of those involved to draw on when transferring knowledge and understandings. For Hargreaves, building social capital involves the development of networks based on mutual trust, within which good practice can spread in natural ways.

Using similar thinking, Talbert and McLaughlin (2002) argue that strong collaborative teacher communities engender 'artisanship' by sustaining teachers' commitment to improving practice. They suggest that this occurs through dialogue and collaboration about ways in which students can be helped to engage, and by sharing and inventing effective classroom practices.

In adopting this thinking, however, it is important to keep in mind the dangers associated with 'groupthink', defined by Janis (1982) as *'a mode of thinking people engage in when they are deeply involved in a cohesive in-group, when the members striving for unanimity override their motivation to realistically appraise alternative courses of action'* (p. 9). This is why an engagement with evidence is so crucial, not least the views of students.

Developing Inclusive Practices

In thinking about the practical implications of these ideas, it is important to note research which suggests that developments in practice are unlikely to occur without some exposure to what teaching actually looks like when it is being done differently (Elmore, Peterson and McCarthy, 1996). Furthermore, this has to be addressed at the individual level before it can be solved at the organisational level (Sammons et al., 2016). Indeed, Lipman (1997) argues that collaboration without attention to changes at the individual level can simply result in teachers coming together to reinforce existing practices, rather than confronting the difficulties they face in different ways

Florian and Black-Hawkins' (2011) important study of how practitioners make sense of a policy of inclusion led them to argue that it is not 'what' but 'how' support is provided that is important. This finding preceded the development of their *'inclusive pedagogical approach'* (Black-Hawkins and Florian, 2012) which argues that assistance can be used to provide rich learning opportunities in ways that are ordinarily available in the community of the class rather than as additional provision for some, different to that which is available to others.

Inclusive pedagogy is an approach to teaching and learning whereby learners' differences are presented as a challenge for teachers to respond to in ways which encourages an open-ended view of students' potential. Difficulties that students may face are understood as factors to be given consideration in learning and teaching. Extending forms of activity in order to widen opportunities for everyone to learn can meet individual needs by encouraging participation and allowing students to monitor their own progress at their own pace within the learning community of the class. The belief underpinning this approach is that every student has potential and will make progress in a different way and at a different pace.

This thinking echoes the ground-breaking *'Learning without Limits'* initiative, which examined ways of teaching that are free from predetermined assumptions about the abilities of students within a class (Hart, 2003; Hart et al., 2004). This involved researchers in working closely with a group of teachers who had rejected ideas of fixed ability in order to study their practice. The researchers started from the belief that constraints are placed on student learning by ability-focused practices that lead children to define themselves in comparison to their peers.

Hart and her colleagues argue that the notion of ability as inborn intelligence has come to be seen as *a natural way of talking about children* that summarises their perceived differences. However, the teachers involved in their research based their practices on a different perspective, one that adopted a belief that things can change and be changed for the better, recognising that whatever a child's present attainments and characteristics, given the right conditions, everybody's capacity for learning can be enhanced. Approaching their work with this mind-set, the teachers involved in the study were seen to analyse gaps between their aspirations for children and what was actually happening.

Using Evidence

At the heart of the processes in schools where changes in practice do occur is the development of a common language with which colleagues can talk to one another and, indeed, to themselves about detailed aspects of their practice (Huberman, 1993). Without such a language, teachers find it very difficult to experiment with new possibilities.

Lefstein, Vedder-Weiss and Segal (2020) point to the importance of the conversations embedded in teachers' day-to-day work, through which they learn from one another what it means to be a teacher and how to perform their duties. These authors explain how professional knowledge and skills, much of which are implicit, are learned on the job, through participation in work practices and informal interactions with colleagues. This means that professional knowledge is intimately related to the practices through which it is constructed and to which it is applied. Given the situated nature of knowledge, ideas constructed with colleagues at school are more likely to be used within a school, whereas ideas constructed within professional development workshops are only likely to be applied in the social practice of participating in such events.

As I have suggested, much of what teachers do during the intensive encounters that occur within classrooms is carried out at an automatic, intuitive level, as they respond to unpredictable events. Furthermore, this goes on in contexts where there is little time to stop and think. This is why having the opportunity to see colleagues at work is so crucial to the success of attempts to develop practice. It is through such shared experiences that colleagues can help one another to articulate what they currently do and define what they might like to do (Hiebert, Gallimore and Stigler, 2002). It is also the means whereby space is created within which taken-for-granted assumptions about particular groups of learners can be subjected to mutual critique, something that is crucial in relation to responding to student diversity.

What is needed, therefore, is a working atmosphere within schools that encourages those involved to generate and analyse evidence regarding the experiences of the students. This requires a degree of risk taking, as suggested by Hargreaves (2003), who argues: *'Unless schools acquire a willingness to take risks, and to learn from the inevitable mistakes, there can be no real innovation at school level'* (p. 36).

Relevant to this, our own research has revealed more about how social learning processes within schools influence people's actions and, indeed, the thinking that informs their actions (Ainscow, Nicolaidou and West, 2003). Often this is stimulated by an engagement with various forms of evidence that create periods of turbulence in relation to existing ways of thinking and working. Particularly powerful techniques in this respect involve the use of mutual observation, sometimes through video recordings, and evidence collected from students about teaching and learning arrangements within a school (Messiou and Ainscow, 2021). Under certain conditions, such approaches provide 'interruptions' that stimulate self-questioning, creativity, and action. In so doing, they sometimes lead to a reframing of perceived problems through processes of reflection that, in turn, draw attention to overlooked possibilities for addressing barriers to participation and learning (Lamote and Engels, 2010; Lewis, Perry and Murata, 2006; Yost, Sentner and Forlenza-Bailey, 2000).

However, none of this provides a straightforward mechanism for the development of more inclusive practices. Any space for reflection that is created as a result of engaging with evidence may sometimes be filled by conflicting agendas. Indeed, our analysis of detailed examples has revealed how deeply held beliefs within schools can prevent the experimentation that is necessary in order to foster the development of more inclusive ways of working (e.g., Ainscow and Howes, 2007; Ainscow and Kaplan, 2005).

Resources

Focusing specifically on finding ways of using professional development to promote inclusive practices, in what follows I consider examples from our recent work in Latin America (see: Ainscow et al.,

2024; Calderón-Almendros et al., 2020). As explained earlier, this programme of research has involved two phases. The first of these involved participatory research experiences in seven Latin American countries (i.e., Chile, Colombia, Ecuador, Mexico, Paraguay, Peru, and Uruguay), and the second phase took the form of collaborative inquiry projects with networks of schools in some of these countries.

The approach used in the school projects was built around the UNESCO-International Bureau of Education resource pack, *'Reaching Out to All Learners'*, that I developed with a group of colleagues from different parts of the world (see https://www.ibe.unesco.org/en/node/103?hub=41). The second edition of these materials, published in a number of languages in March 2022, is intended to influence and support inclusive thinking and practices at all levels of an education system.

The materials are based on the following definitions proposed in UNESCO guidance (2017) that I referred to earlier:

- **Inclusion** is a process that helps overcome barriers limiting the presence, participation, and achievement of learners; and
- **Equity** is about ensuring that there is a concern with fairness, such that the education of all learners is seen as having equal importance.

As I have stressed, these definitions involve a move away from explanations of educational failure that concentrate on the characteristics of individual children and their families, towards an analysis of contextual barriers experienced by students within schools. In this way, students who do not respond to existing arrangements come to be regarded as 'hidden voices' who, under certain conditions, can encourage the improvement of schools (Ainscow, 2024a).

Drawing on the findings of the projects described in earlier chapters, the *Reaching Out to All Learners* materials address the practicalities of applying these ideas in schools, including early years and further education provision. More specifically, the materials focus on three strategic questions:

- How can schools be developed in order to respond positively to student diversity?

- How can classroom practices be developed that will ensure that lessons are inclusive?
- How can practitioners engage families, partner schools, and the wider community in their efforts to become inclusive and equitable?

Whilst the resource pack can be read by individuals, it has been designed to encourage collaborative forms of professional learning in the following settings:

- Within individual or groups of schools to promote the development of policies and practices;
- As part of in-service courses or workshops for teachers;
- Within collaborative action research projects involving schools working with the support of university staff; and
- Within pre-service teacher education courses.

The materials involve a focus on:

- **Clarity of meaning** – The resource pack seeks to promote the development of new ways of addressing diversity among learners. Within the materials, much importance is attached to the need for a common understanding of the purposes of this approach.
- **Analysis of contexts** – The aim is to draw attention to and find ways of overcoming aspects of current thinking, policy, and practice that may be creating barriers to the presence, participation, and achievement of some children and young people.
- **Building on existing practices** – Recognising that there are usually effective practices that can be built upon within any context, the processes recommended in the resource pack encourage the exchange of expertise within and between schools, and with families and the wider community.
- **Working collaboratively** – Rethinking practice in relation to inclusion and equity is likely to involve periods of 'turbulence', as business-as-usual ideas are challenged. The materials therefore emphasise the importance of promoting mutual support among stakeholders.

- **Evaluating progress** – As the resource pack is used, there is a need to collect evidence regarding the use and impact of the changes that are introduced. This can also help in ensuring effective implementation.
- **Managing change** – The use of the resource pack has to be managed and led collectively. Thus, the materials stress the importance of strengthening leadership practice at all levels, including the classroom level.

It must be noted that the *Reaching Out to All Learners* resource pack is intended to be used flexibly in response to culturally diverse contexts that are at different stages of development and where resources vary considerably. With this in mind, extensive use is made of examples from different parts of the world to encourage the development of new ways of including all students.

The accounts that follow are of schools that took part in programmes of professional development in various countries in Latin America (Ainscow et al., 2024). These involved me in working with colleagues in networks of schools. In each context sections of the resource pack were selected and adapted to suit local contexts. As with our earlier projects, each participating school created staff inquiry teams to lead a process of collaborative inquiry and professional development.

Focusing on Practice

This first example took place in the city of Santiago, Chile, and was led by my colleague Cynthia Duk from the University Central of Chile. It involved her in developing a collaborative alliance with the local education authority in the commune of Peñalolen. The purpose of this partnership was to explore how teachers can be helped to respond to multiple challenges in complex educational environments with high diversity of students (Duk et al., 2021).

The population that attends the 15 public schools of Peñalolén has a large proportion of students from disadvantaged socio-economic backgrounds, as well as indigenous students and migrants from other

Latin American countries. In addition, all the schools have integration programmes to support disabled learners.

The initiative took place over three years, with the participation of 120 professionals: principals, teachers, and support staff. The main objective was to promote positive attitudes and dispositions towards the development of inclusive classrooms, where all students feel recognised and valued equally, and benefit from educational experiences that ensure their participation and learning.

To encourage the involvement of the schools an initial meeting was held with principals to explain the programme and receive suggestions as to how it might be made relevant. It was also crucial to establish an agreement about time and type of facilities required to carry out effective collaborative action research processes. Three to six teachers per school were invited to participate. In this way, it was ensured that each school could create one or two staff inquiry teams. In order to begin the process, a workshop was held with the objective of presenting the methodology, its meaning and foundations and benefits, as well as practical procedures.

Among the strategies from the resource pack introduced to participants was a form of lesson study, a systematic procedure for the development of teaching that is well established in Japan and some other Asian countries (Lewis, Perry and Murata, 2006). This involves trios of teachers working together to improve the effectiveness of the experiences that teachers provide for all of their students. The core activity involves collaborative research on a shared area of focus that is generated through discussion. The content of this focus is the planned lesson, which is then used as the basis of gathering data on the quality of experience that students receive. These are called *research lessons* and are used to examine the responsiveness of the students to the planned activities. Within the programme, this approach was viewed positively by many of the teachers due to its positive impact on the development of more inclusive practices

Within the approach to lesson study recommended in the resource pack each member of the trio has the opportunity to experience different roles: planning, teaching, observing, analysing, and providing feedback to make the class more inclusive. The implementation of the approach had the support of university facilitators, who made visits to each school to observe practices and offer feedback based on evidence.

Once the trios of teachers were formed, each team defined the grade, subject(s), and thematic unit that they would work on, as well as the schedule of classes to be implemented. They then went on to discuss the diversity that characterises the chosen group of students, reflecting on the following questions: How can we ensure that all students in the class are motivated, participate, and learn? How can we make our classes more inclusive?

With this agenda in mind, the teachers planned a learning unit that would be followed by their three classes. They also considered how they could collect the opinions of their students to inform their planning of the research lesson.

Reflecting on this process, one teacher commented

> It expanded the conception of diversity in my mind; for me it had to do with students with special needs but I realized that it includes cultural and socioeconomic contexts. We are all different - it is the reality that you have in the classroom and that changed my vision.

In teaching the research lesson, one colleague leads the class while the other two observe and keep a record, focusing on student responses: What has motivated them? How have they participated in the activities? How have they interacted with each other? What support have they required?

In discussing their involvement, a teacher commented:

> One of the strongest and most important reflections we made was that there are students who can spend 'eternity' in the classroom as if they did not exist.

A member of the same trio reflected:

> The opportunity of being in the classroom and seeing the three of us as 'the teacher', seeing the children in the class dynamics, seeing how the children reacted to the various strategies, I think without a doubt enriches our classroom practices.

Following each of the research lessons the trios analysed the experience in order to improve the plan for the next class, which is taught by another teacher in the team. A central element for improvement is observation-based peer review. A teacher commented on this:

> We listened to the students and offered them three different activities with the same objective, where they had to decide. That class was the most enriching, because we felt that they were participants in our planning, and that really helped me change my way of seeing, planning and assessment.

At the end of this process the trios reflected on the implications of the experience: What have we learned about inclusive practice and collaborative work? How did considering students' voices help us? What can we do to generalise this process across our school? This led one teacher to comment:

> We learned the impact of systematically collecting the views of the students and making this instance something more than just asking what would you like to learn and how. We realized that by expanding the ways of asking we can obtain more and more specific information, transforming this process into a valuable opportunity to improve.

Finally, it should be noted that the value that many of the teachers attributed to this experience was the opportunity it gave them to reflect on their teaching collectively and address problems associated with their practice through collaborative inquiry amongst peers, plus the external views of the university facilitators. In this sense, practitioners highlighted the contribution of lesson study as a powerful resource for collaborative professional learning, which allowed them to expand their previous conceptions of diversity; explore new strategies for responding to differences; become aware of the importance of the student's voice to make the class more inclusive; and move the attention from teaching to student participation and learning.

Addressing Barriers

This second experience was part of programme of professional development funded by the Secretariat of Education of the Government of the State of San Luis Potosí, Mexico. It took the form of a process of collaborative action research in which my colleague Ignacio Calderon from the University of Malaga and I used sections of the UNESCO resource pack with school staff and professional support teams external to the schools.

The objective of the programme was to address the challenge of inclusion within the schools through the use of a strategy in which evidence was collected to stimulate improvements in policies, organisation, and practices. This involved students, teachers, and principals as active partners in the implementation and evaluation process. The programme took place between June and November 2023.

This account refers to one of the schools, which has 354 students and 21 teachers. The process there began with an analysis that the school usually makes at the beginning of each school year of the students' academic progress, behaviour, and previous learning levels, plus the assessments of support staff, particularly referring to those students seen as having special needs. Reflecting on this analysis led to a research focus: *a concern that these students should feel more part of the rest of their groups at school.*

Among the methodological strategies used in the process, a staff inquiry group developed surveys for parents, interviews with students, recording the interventions of some of them to know their perspectives on their teachers' performance and the school, and relationships within the school. Workshops were also developed to understand the levels of participation that students perceive, with the idea of giving staff a more faithful image of their teaching practices. As with the schools in Chile, use was also made of lesson study to develop inclusive practices.

Among the findings, some of the students labelled as having special needs said that they often felt strange, as if they were not part of the group, and even felt ignored by their teachers because they did not pay them the same attention as their classmates. Some of these students also commented that teachers did not seem to believe or even trust them. This led a support teacher to comment

> These students did not feel part of their group. They cried when talking about their experiences at school.

When students took part in interviews that revealed these feelings, some of the teachers became distressed. This continued during a meeting that provided opportunities for teachers to know more about how the students felt at school. The teachers then began to share their concern about something of which they had been largely unaware, generating a greater desire to improve communication with students, empathy, and inclusion. The school principal agreed with those teachers who argued that the evidence required changes in practices that recognised errors in the way that some students had been treated.

All of this had important repercussions for teaching and learning processes, which underwent significant changes. For example, some of the teachers were fascinated by the rapid progress in reading and writing made by one of the boys after having felt that he was being listened to and that the teachers were trying to transform his feelings of being undervalued. This suggested that certain changes in teacher attitudes can lead to improvements in academic development and participation with the rest of the classmates. In this way, teachers learnt to value the importance of seeking the views of students and families. The school principal commented:

> Personally, it has meant a slap, because we thought we were an inclusive school. And I have learned that it is a process that you have to stick with. It is not applying a project, but maintaining it. The greatest learning has come from the words of students, families and teachers to see how we feel, to go from there recognizing that we do not know everything. It left me anxious to continue preparing.

In this school, taking into account of the preferences, interests, and comments of children had a significant impact on the teachers, who had previously made decisions regardless of the opinions of their students. This was something they admitted that they did without any intention, believing it was the right thing to do. This raised awareness was caused by listening to the children. Through this process they were able to realise that, as teachers, they focused too much attention on learning outcomes, but this was not enough, since students' emotions greatly impact on their learning. This led one teacher to comment:

> We realized that we are a barrier, and we thought that the barriers were something else and were in other places. We commonly say: he has cognitive problems, or he has, he has, he has ... And now we don't.

For their part, some of the support teachers became aware that removing students from their classrooms to attend to them in a segregated setting was a mistake, even though well intended. This led the support teachers to look for responses so that the students would feel part of their class. Meanwhile, the teachers worked together to develop ways of involving all students in their lessons. In this process, they confirmed that it is possible to educate the entire group together, without separating students by abilities.

Leaving No One behind

This third account is from Uruguay. It describes how, over a year, secondary schools participated in a network that carried out collaborative action research based on the UNESCO resource pack (Ainscow and Viola, 2023). The overall goal was to throw light on those students who are at risk of being left behind, and to plan, implement, and evaluate actions to prevent this from happening.

Using a specially adapted set of the UNESCO resource materials, Mercedes Viola and I supported six secondary schools in using collaborative action research to make better use of the existing expertise of their teachers. The schools were diverse in terms of their location in the country, as well as the nature of the populations they serve and the roles they fulfil within the education system.

For example, one of the project schools, located in the city of Florida, has 426 students, 12–15 years old. They come from all the city's neighbourhoods as well as the outskirts, and from a wide range of socioeconomic and cultural backgrounds. The school has 17 classes, across two shifts, and a staff of 78 teachers.

An inquiry team of teachers and support staff was created with the aim of improving the inclusion of all students in the school through a focus on wellbeing and enjoyment, and by promoting their involvement and commitment. To identify those most at risk of being left behind the team reviewed available information on students' educational pathways, and had exchanges with teachers, coordinators, and pedagogical consultants. A target group of students was then identified. They included young people seen as having anxieties, autism spectrum disorders, socialising challenges, behavioural challenges, or little or no support from their families, plus some high-performing students who do not socialise.

An anonymous online survey was designed and implemented with the aim of knowing the students' emotions and feelings regarding the school, adults and peers, and home circumstances. This was seen as an opportunity to *'pause… reflect… look… and see ourselves'*.

The responses were classified into three categories: students' contexts, institutional factors, and a subjective dimension regarding the student's relationship with their peers and teachers. Based on the findings, some activities were planned to generate more information, including two participatory workshops to explore some emotional dimensions. In these contexts, the aim was to reflect on mutual respect, tolerance, fellowship, collaboration, and team organisation.

The workshops were developed in cooperation with students, teachers of different subjects and levels, as well as subject coordinators. A rubric and a worksheet were designed to observe group dynamics, focusing on engagement, peer listening, contributions, and conversations. After some reflections in small groups, posters were created to synthesise these reflections. These posters were displayed on hallway walls.

To involve the whole education community and families, the staff team decided to organise an event in the local streets. This allowed the school to go out into the neighbourhood and engage with the community at large, as well as show what students feel, think, and do. The activity was designed around themes, characters, and cultures, and was carried out through collaborative teams, including parents who helped in organising the event. This event was covered by the local press, which provided a further opportunity to collect the views of some of the families, who said they were very happy to take part and to be able to promote teamwork and give support to their children, since they considered the ties created between the school and families to be crucial.

Participation in the whole project was strong, which indicated a genuine interest and commitment to improve within the school. The various activities used were carried out collaboratively and constructively. In this way, those within the school were able to re-examine some aspects of policy and practice. As a result of their participation some of the team members felt they had undergone personal growth.

The process was seen as enriching in all aspects – research, reflection, exchange, and action – both for the staff inquiry team and through collaboration with students, teachers, and families. Looking to the future, the team have an expectation that the project will seed multiple future changes within their school.

Challenges

Accounts such as these, alongside many others (see Ainscow, 2024a), lead me to argue that there is massive untapped potential for promoting inclusive practices within schools. They also throw light on the changes needed in order to mobilise this potential and the sorts of contextual challenges that are likely to inhibit efforts to make such changes. In particular, they suggest a series of strategies that are required in order to use professional development to promote inclusion.

Within the projects, progress was most evident in those schools where those leading improvement efforts had the backing of key players, particularly senior members of staff. In some schools, we saw how the strong support and involvement of principals and senior staff led to a rich process, while those schools that did not have that support often experienced challenges. In other cases, whilst some teachers wanted to continue but without the support of the principal they could not find the way to do it. This suggests that in moving forward there is a need to identify and engage the support of those who can make things happen, as well as those who might block things from happening.

A key issue that emerged during the projects was the difficulty in finding time for reflection and collaborative work. Meanwhile, the frequent rotation of principals and changes in teaching teams in some of the countries was seen to hinder the continuity of the process of transforming the culture of educational centres towards inclusion. This reminds us that spaces for collaboration to take place are crucial in order to sustain cultural transformation.

Within Latin American countries, where government officials at the national and regional levels tend to have considerable influence, their support is particularly important. The introduction of the approaches I describe requires them to adjust their ways of working in response to the development of improvement strategies that are led from within schools. In taking on such new roles, government officials at the national and regional levels can position themselves as *the conscience of the system*: guardians of improved outcomes for all young people and their families, and champions of a more collaborative approach. All of this points to the importance of organisational cultures.

Changing School Cultures

The social psychologist Edgar Schein (1985) suggests that cultures are about the deeper levels of basic assumptions and beliefs that are shared by members of an organisation, operating unconsciously to define how they view themselves and their working context. Writing more specifically about educational contexts, David Hargreaves (1995) argues that cultures can be seen as having a reality-defining function, enabling those within an institution to make sense of themselves, their actions, and their environment. A current reality-defining function of culture, he suggests, is often a problem-solving function inherited from the past. This leads Hargreaves to conclude that by examining the reality-defining aspects of a culture it should be possible to gain a better understanding of the routines the organisation has developed in response to the tasks it faces. The implication is that barriers experienced in implementing programmes of professional development within schools may be as a result of bumping up against taken-for-granted assumptions.

Further theoretical perspectives relevant to our understanding of these experiences are provided by the idea of 'communities of practice', as developed by Etienne Wenger (1998). He explains practice in terms of those things that individuals within a community do, drawing on available resources to further a set of shared goals. This goes beyond how practitioners complete their tasks, to include, for example, how they make it through the day, commiserating about the pressures and constraints within which they have to operate. Practices are thus ways of negotiating meaning through social action, which underlines the importance of the conversations embedded in the day-to-day work of practitioners.

In explaining this process, Wenger argues that communities 'reify' their practices by producing representations of them, such as tools, symbols, rules, and documents (and even catchphrases). However, these reifications have to be given meaning through a process of participation, which consists of the shared experiences and negotiations that result from social interaction within a purposive community. It follows that 'outsiders', such as me, are likely to find it difficult to make sense of what we observe and hear about these processes.

Wenger offers some helpful guidelines for judging whether a particular social collective can be considered as a community of practice. Since such a community involves mutual engagement, a negotiated enterprise, and a repertoire of resources and practices, then its members should be expected to:

- Interact more intensively with, and know more about, others in the group than those outside the group;
- Hold their actions accountable (and be willing for others in the community to hold them accountable) more to the group's joint enterprise than to some other enterprise;
- Be more able to evaluate the actions of other members of the group than the actions of those outside the group; and
- Draw on locally produced resources and artefacts to negotiate meaning, more so than those that are imported from outside the group.

By these criteria, an educational system can be seen as a complex network of interconnected communities of practices within (and sometimes across) schools. All of this suggests that improvement agendas of the sort I have described cannot simply be imposed. Specifically, proposals for change, however powerfully enforced, have to be endowed with meaning within local contexts before they can inform practice. This implies that schools (or, at least, the communities of practice within schools) may well negotiate local meanings for those agendas that are different from those of the formulators themselves or, indeed, of other local schools.

The Nature of Practice

There is one further factor at work, which may be more fundamental. We are familiar with the notion that professionals operate in arenas characterised by complexity and uncertainty, such that their practice must constantly adjust to new and unique situations (Eraut, 1994; Schön, 2017). As Eraut notes, this creates a significant problem, given the tendency of human actors to routinise their actions:

> The development of routines is a natural process, essential for coping with the job and responsible for increased efficiency; but the combination of tacit knowledge and intuitive decision-making makes them difficult to monitor and to keep under critical control. As a result, routines tend to become progressively dysfunctional over time; not only do they fail to adjust to new circumstances but 'shortcuts' gradually intrude, some of which only help professionals to cope with pressure at the expense of their clients.
>
> (Eraut, 1994, pp. 111–112)

The 'clients' of teachers are, of course, their students. However, not only are students active participants in the schooling process – making their views and feelings known, sometimes in no uncertain terms – but the aim of teaching is to elicit some sort of response from them, whether that be in the form of long-term outcomes or immediate classroom behaviours.

If, as Eraut suggests, teachers' routines become progressively dysfunctional, then the desired responses from students will fail to materialise. This situation will be exacerbated where students are less reluctant to make their dissatisfaction known to their teachers, and where teachers and schools are held tightly to account for delivering certain sorts of outcomes.

The implication of all this is that there is an in-built dynamic within schools which brings teachers face-to-face with a mismatch between their routinised practices and the actual responses of their students. If inclusion is understood as a process of reducing barriers to participation and learning, then it seems reasonable to suggest that this in-built dynamic also brings teachers face-to-face with the non-inclusive nature of their practices.

If we then go on to see school staffs as consisting of communities of practice, we can see how a core task of such groups is to develop shared meanings (and therefore practices) around the recurrent experience of mismatch between established practices and the realities of their students. This does not mean, of course, that every mismatch will be acknowledged as an anomaly, or that the shared meanings that are developed around them will lead to more inclusive practices. However, it does mean that fundamental questions about inclusiveness arise and can potentially be made explicit as a matter of course in every school, regardless of whether or not those involved espouse a rhetoric of inclusion.

Our work suggests that this is not a merely theoretical possibility. In some of our project schools, we saw how a mismatch between established practices and the actual outcomes of that practice became apparent. This might relate to a group of students whose exclusion from classrooms ceases to be taken for granted, or those who disrupt established practices, or students who fail to reach desired targets. We have also worked with schools where shifting demographics produced student intakes that responded differently to the schools' traditional population, or classrooms in which individual students seemed to be doing less well than their teachers hoped, or experiences of new practices which suggested to teachers that their students could do better if they abandoned their existing ways of working.

Leading School Developments

The experiences described in this chapter involve moves away from an analysis of learner deficiencies towards a concern with contextual barriers that are limiting the participation and achievement of students. As such, the aim is to eliminate social exclusion that is a consequence of attitudes and responses to diversity in race, social class, ethnicity, religion, gender, and abilities.

All of this has implications for the ways in which the transformation of implicit ideas, languages, cultures, and practices related to inclusion and equity can be achieved, not least by paying attention to the care of those involved. This means that teachers and others involved in the education of young people must be supported in moving beyond what I referred to earlier as deeply held beliefs that can prevent experimentation. In this way, practitioners can reconceptualise the actions of their school beyond taken-for-granted assumptions that lead to a perception that there are no opportunities to do anything different.

The implication is that professional development activities must involve an 'ethics of care' (Felder, 2021). With this in mind, developing systematic dialogue and listening processes, such as those that I have witnessed in schools, enable those involved to humanise educational relationships (Freire, 1972). In the school contexts I have described, this often led to a particular emphasis on taking account of student views.

All of this involves a recognition that identities, both professional and personal, are reformulated in the processes of reification and participation that Wenger describes in his analysis of communities of practice. This can also have an impact on the subjective constructions of teachers about their students. For example, reifications in reference to students labelled as 'having special needs' are likely to limit the responses of teachers, as well as creating a ceiling for those learners who are so reified. It is only through the expansion of participation that these borders begin to move.

In relation to this argument my colleague Ignacio Calderon drew my attention to the Mexican school as an instructive example. He explained that the collaborative action research there led to a realisation that the barriers were not within the children but related to the teachers' own thinking and practices. And this, in turn, implies that children can learn what was not within their scope as previously reified within the institution. All of this is about transforming the implicit personal and professional assumptions, which must go through a process of rethinking, leading to experimentation with new ways of working.

In referring to such approaches, leadership expert Viviane Robinson and her colleagues (2008) note that taking part in collaborative enquiries into improving teaching and learning is the most impactful action a school leader can take to improve educational outcomes for students. It follows that leadership is a factor in making this happen.

Certain forms of leadership are known to be effective in promoting inclusion in education (Riehl, 2000). These approaches focus attention on teaching and learning; they create strong supportive communities of students, teachers, and parents; they nurture the understanding of a culture of education among families; and, they involve multi-agency support.

Conclusion

Whilst the developments described in this chapter were set in various parts of Latin America, the ideas presented about using professional development to promote inclusive practices are relevant to other parts of the world, not least because of the emphasis placed on the importance of contextual analysis. Moreover, the sorts of ideas to support implementation of inclusive thinking I have set out continue to impact on efforts to guide educational improvements in both the developed and developing world (Ainscow, 2024a).

The implication is that significant changes have to be made in the way education systems operate in order to create the organisational conditions within which new thinking can be accommodated. And, teacher professional development has to be at the heart of efforts to create self-improving schools. In particular, the starting point involves building on existing practices.

Therefore, my third proposition is that *schools should become learning communities where the development of all members is encouraged and supported*. This requires sustained efforts within schools, recognising that changing outcomes for vulnerable students are unlikely to be achieved unless there are changes in the attitudes, beliefs, and actions of adults. As I have argued, the starting point must therefore be with practitioners: enlarging their capacity to imagine what might be achieved, and increasing their sense of accountability for bringing this about. This may also involve tackling negative assumptions, most often relating to expectations about certain groups of learners and their capabilities.

5
MOVING KNOWLEDGE AROUND

The approach to reform outlined so far is based on the idea of those within schools collecting and engaging with various forms of evidence in order to stimulate moves to create more inclusive ways of working. The studies I have summarised provide encouraging evidence of the potential of this approach. They also throw light on the difficulties in putting such thinking into practice, particularly within policy contexts that put pressure on schools to compete. This points to some of the limitations of within-school strategies, suggesting that these should be complemented with efforts to encourage greater cooperation amongst schools.

It is important to realise, however, that developing partnerships between schools is not a straightforward process. Too often it can lead to meetings without any significant action. For example, in the networks referred to in earlier chapters, schools were encouraged to visit one another in order to generate evidence regarding their shared focus on developing more inclusive practices. However, these visits were not always successful. This seemed to be particularly so when the host teachers interpreted the visits solely as opportunities for the visitors to learn. On these occasions, the hosts positioned themselves as teachers rather than learners. Typically, the visit then consisted of a demonstration of various teaching strategies that had been judged to be successful, usually followed by a short question and answer session. On these occasions, those receiving the visit merely rehearsed what they already knew and responded to questions beyond the procedural as if they were challenges, rather than openings for debate.

On the other hand, successful visits were usually characterised by a sense of mutual learning amongst hosts and visitors. It was noticeable, too, that the focus for these visits often took some time to identify and clarify. Indeed, the preliminary negotiations that took place were in themselves a key aspect of the process.

The English Context

Once again, England provides an interesting context to explore this agenda. Despite successive government initiatives with the declared intent of addressing equity and social justice, significant numbers of children and young people remain marginalised within or excluded from schools. Meanwhile, the increasing trend of placement in various forms of alternative provision adds to the marginalisation of some and often the more vulnerable learners, while placing further pressure on local authority resources.

The coronavirus pandemic threw new light on these challenges. In particular, it showed how, despite the efforts of schools and local authorities, it was the most vulnerable learners who experienced the greatest impact in relation to their engagement in schools and progress in learning.

England is also typical of many countries in having strong spatial concentrations of poverty and poor educational outcomes. These typically occur in places with weak physical, economic, and service infrastructures for addressing poor educational outcomes. For one of the wealthiest nations on the planet, this is a source of national shame. It also serves to remind us that decades of centralised reform, that have weakened local democratic influence and have thereby had the effect of fragmenting the school system, have done much more to reinforce rather than address these concerns. All of this points to the need for locally coordinated efforts to promote more equitable and socially just forms of education within particular places.

The initiatives I describe in this chapter to develop such efforts have taken place within a policy context that places an emphasis on competition between schools as a strategy for achieving improvements. A major strand in this policy direction has been the rapid expansion of the academies programme.

Independent State Schools

Academies were launched in the year 2001 with the aim of replacing inner-city secondary schools that were defined as requiring 'special measures' as a result of being inspected. What was distinctive about the early academies was that, although they were state-funded, they became autonomous from local authority control, had their own sponsor, and were given greater freedom regarding the national curriculum and national agreements on teachers' pay and conditions.

Since the earlier initiatives, the academies programme has undergone considerable changes and growth. Following the election of the Conservative-led coalition government in 2010, and then the Conservative government in 2015, it moved from targeting urban secondary schools seen as 'failing', to a system-wide structural change causing seismic shifts in the English education landscape. Writing about this reform, Eyles and Machin (2015) comment:

> The academies programme that has been undertaken in English education is turning out to be one of the most radical and encompassing programmes of school reform that has been seen in the recent past in advanced countries.
>
> (p. 1)

An independent Commission set up to review these developments pointed out that the original aim of academies was *'to address entrenched failure in schools with low performance, most particularly, schools located in the most disadvantaged parts of the country'* (Husbands et al., 2013, p. 4). Since then, the focus has changed towards increasing the autonomy of all schools and setting up new academies throughout the country. These developments are set within a policy context in which the dominant model has become schools linking together in multi-academy trusts (MATs), with oversight coming from national rather than local government.

As a result of this expanding academies programme, the education system in England has become increasingly diverse. Furthermore, the introduction of various other types of schools that operate under the academy legislation – such as free schools, studio schools, and university technical colleges – has contributed to the complexity of the scene.

All of which suggests that autonomous schools are well on the way to becoming *the* system of English state education, which makes it a particularly challenging context within which to encourage school partnerships.

Encouraging Developments

A recent study that I carried out in England with my University of Manchester colleagues, Paul Armstrong, Bee Hughes, and Stephen Rayner, set out to explore what form school partnerships might take and some of the systemic barriers to such cooperation. It provided an independent, evidence-based analysis of a series of existing innovations within the field that are underpinned by locally instigated partnerships (Ainscow et al., 2023).

The study was commissioned by the Staff College, an organisation which supports the development of leadership and management capacity in local authorities and their partners and, through this, contributes to the improvement of locality services for children, young people, and families. Anton Florek from the Staff College advised on the setting up and analysis of the research.

Building on the findings of earlier research carried out by Christine Gilbert (2018), our study analysed developments in eight well-established area school partnership initiatives in order to address the following research questions:

- What are the conditions that facilitate the establishment of school partnerships?
- What are the features and benefits of these partnerships?
- What barriers do they face and how are these being addressed?
- What are the implications for the creation of effective forms of local coordination within education systems?

The research focused on examples from across England, some of which involve partnerships within local authorities, whilst others are area or regionally focused.

An initial phase of data collection comprised a national survey of senior school leaders and local authority personnel. This informed the design of a second phase involving case studies of eight partnerships in which data were generated via documentary analysis and focused interviews with a sample of stakeholders.

This evidence was then used to produce an initial account of each partnership. In order to establish the credibility of these accounts, initial drafts were negotiated with respondents during a seminar organised in each context. This process was intended to inform thinking within the field so as to help move practice forward.

Field work was carried out by the members of our research team, all of whom have extensive experience of carrying out research within education systems. They also have a history of working closely with policy-makers and practitioners in using research findings to guide strategic decision-making. To ensure that the research was relevant to current concerns the Staff College created an advisory group, which contributed to the planning of the study, including responding to interim findings.

Once agreed, the case study accounts were further analysed by our team using the research questions as a framework and linking the findings to relevant international research literature. To strengthen the findings, additional information and intelligence were drawn from existing contacts the research team have with other area partnerships, in England and elsewhere.

Market Forces

As I have explained, the last 20 years have seen an increased policy emphasis in England on the power of market forces as a strategy for educational improvement. Whilst this approach has the potential to open up possibilities to inject new energy into the improvement of schools, there is growing evidence from a range of countries that it can lead to increased segregation within education systems (Salokangas and Ainscow, 2017). In the English context, this has further disadvantaged some learners from economically poorer backgrounds and other vulnerable groups, not least those children and young people from black and Asian-heritage backgrounds, and those recently arrived in the country.

These developments have led to what might be described as an educational market-place where schools compete with each other for students. Meanwhile, parents can exercise choice over where their children go to school, often on the basis of inspection grades and student assessment scores.

Coupled with the emphasis on policies fostering greater diversity of schools, this has created a quasi-selective system in which the poorest children tend to attend the lowest-performing schools and make much slower educational progress than their less disadvantaged peers (Kerr and Ainscow, 2022). At the same time, there are worries that these policy moves are loosening the links between schools and their local communities, a factor that is known to be crucial to the promotion of inclusion and equity. It is also the case, however, that this policy has created a context that is encouraging innovations to improve educational outcomes.

All of this raises questions regarding the local coordination of the system. Indeed, this is one of the most worrying aspects of the current English policy context, with its emphasis on school autonomy, competition, and new governance structures that can discourage schools from working with others. A further factor is that recent years have seen a progressively steep decline in the power and influence of local authorities that have traditionally taken on the responsibility of coordination and monitoring of provision. This means that in many parts of the country no single organisation has the oversight that would enable them to orchestrate more collaborative ways of working and to intervene when things go wrong, either within a school or in the performance of its duties towards the local community it serves.

Lessons from the Field

The eight partnerships within our study have different precursors. Each had emerged from a complex policy context, a fragmented education system, and the seeming decline of the role of local government in educational matters. It is important to note, too, that they all have significant involvement of experienced school leaders.

In terms of governance, all of the partnerships have some form of chief executive officer, overseen by a board made up of school leaders, local authority officers, and other (often high profile) educational stakeholders from the region. In some cases, there is an independent chair, a factor that is seen as being of significance. The partnerships are typically funded through a combination of income generated from membership and subscription fees, and specific commissions sourced either from the Government or through focused strategies commissioned by the local authority

Our sample included a remarkably diverse range of formats and styles of working. Some partnerships had been instigated by a local authority, which continues to take on a key coordinating role. For example, one city-wide partnership was described *'as the brainchild of the then children's services director'*. Others involved a local authority in commissioning a separate entity to coordinate the partnership, as well as providing support services to schools. This was described by the lead of a rural partnership as *'a joint enterprise between [our] schools and the council'*, whereas another smaller borough-wide partnership is referred to as a *'family of schools'*, that allows the local authority to delegate key functions and accountabilities. In two cases, there was no evidence of local authority involvement.

At the same time, there were notable commonalities between the different cases. For example, all the partnerships had been instigated 'on the ground' without a central government mandate and in response to a perceived need for such a structure to support the local school system. For example, we heard how partnerships were established *'in the face of shrinking local government'*, or to create a *'culture of collaboration and mutual support amongst [our] schools to ensure the best possible outcomes for all of our region's young people'*. Another was described as a *'partnership vehicle'*, that is *'more than just a casual or loosely framed arrangement but involves real accountability, real structure'*.

Key Features

Across the sample of partnerships the following features were noticeable:

Contexts

What was most striking about all the partnerships is the importance of particular local factors in shaping the ways in which patterns of engagement have developed. In this respect, size is a factor: in some cases, the partnerships began with a small group of schools and then gradually grew.

Some of the partnerships involve schools from more than one local authority, whilst others are clearly focused within the boundaries of particular local authorities. Their perceived strengths were illustrated by one school leader who commented that members recognised:

> It was our network, you know: What is it that we are interested in? And what is it that we want us to work on?

For many colleagues, all of this was seen to involve sharing a 'moral purpose'.

There was also evidence of how earlier national time-limited initiatives, such as City Challenge, had influenced the developments, not least through the continuation of well-established professional and social links between school leaders. This reminds us of how such developments can sometimes have a longer-term impact which may be unrecognised.

Relationships

Across the examples, relationships between the partners were clearly of importance. A useful theoretical interpretation that can be made of this factor is that it seeks to strengthen 'social capital', something that is known to be a feature of education systems that are more able to foster greater equity (Mulford, 2007).

Here, again, local factors were seen to be significant. In particular, we heard how particular individuals or groups of colleagues had taken on leadership roles. It was noticeable, too, that these relationships were linked to contextual factors. In one partnership, for example, a headteacher from a rural partnership explained that the fact that housing in the area was relatively cheap acted as 'a trap', such that many of the senior people involved had worked together over many years.

The pattern of long-serving local headteachers, including senior staff from MATs, getting involved in the development of the partnerships was particularly noticeable. Going forward, this points to a factor that could be encouraged by national policy. That is to say, incentives could be provided to encourage experienced school leaders to take on a wider role of facilitating efforts to coordinate collaboration across local education systems to address challenges in relation to equity. This had happened in some of the earlier projects I have described through the designation of some headteachers as 'system leaders'.

Key Individuals

We were struck by the way that particular people had developed significant leadership roles within their partnerships. Usually, these were long-serving school leaders. However, in a few instances, senior local authority staff were seen as key figures.

As well as providing leadership within their partnerships, some of these individuals had established strong links with regional and national officials. This sometimes enabled them to access additional support for their partnerships. Talking about these links, one senior local authority officer explained that her regular contact with government officials helped her to coordinate an interpretation of national policy changes that were relevant to her local context.

At the same time, these key individuals are sometimes consulted about possible national policy developments. In these ways, they seem to be creating useful informal networks within a policy context in which national policy-makers and those in the field have tended to become rather disconnected. This means that these key players can be seen as taking on the roles of what has been defined as 'policy entrepreneurs' (Hughes, 2019).

Values

It was noticeable that all the partnerships had established some form of statement of principles to guide their efforts. These were often articulated through their websites. The purpose of these statements varied from place to place. In some instances, they seemed to be mainly there as a form of background rhetoric, rarely mentioned in relation to what the partnerships are doing. In other cases, however, those involved made frequent reference to the value statements as they addressed particular decisions regarding actions to be taken about priorities and how resources were to be mobilised. In one instance, we were told how representatives from prospective new partner schools were interviewed in relation to their commitment to the values agreed within the partnership.

The statements, plus other publicity regarding the work of a partnership, also helped to encourage schools to join. Interestingly, the headteacher of a school facing challenging circumstances explained that some of his *'middle class parents'* had encouraged him to get involved in the partnership. He went on to describe the way that the partners had provided tangible efforts to *'turn the school round'* through sharing improvement strategies, such as staff coaching.

The Use of Evidence

Given the particular focus on addressing the challenge of equity, we saw this as being a crucial agenda for our enquiries. With this in mind, at some point during each of our focus group meetings, we asked partners to explain who would know if a school was getting into difficulty in some way and what actions would be taken. In general, we were surprised at the responses we received, with many partnerships seeming to make limited use of data to determine their priorities.

In some cases, however, it was clear that the groups coordinating the partnerships had established ways of addressing this agenda, not least through their engagement with evidence. Where difficulties were seen to arise, action was then taken to coordinate relevant support from within the partnership, or by mobilising external support. In some of these situations, the involvement of local authority officers with their wider knowledge of the local school system was significant in facilitating these interventions.

In the small number of cases where evidence was being used effectively, statistical patterns in relation to factors such as student outcomes, attendance and exclusions, interpreted through local intelligence, were seen to focus planning and action within the partnership. This afforded such partnerships the kind of oversight that is necessary to ensure no school goes without support when it is required.

Challenges

Whilst we were not in a position to evaluate the impact of the partnerships systematically, we did gain some sense of the degree to which they are effective from our discussions with stakeholders. In some cases, we were also provided with data that pointed to impacts in relation to indicators such as student progress, attendance, exclusions, and inspection reports.

In those examples that seemed to be working well, we saw evidence of the impact of the factors reported in the previous section. At the same time, we became aware of factors that make effective partnerships more difficult to achieve. Once again, these factors tend to be context specific. However, the following features were evident to varying degrees across our sample.

School Diversity

In all cases, the issue of the diversity of schools within a local area was seen as a challenge and, in some contexts, a significant barrier to progress. For example, we were given accounts of where MATs were said to have discouraged their academies from joining a partnership on the basis that necessary support was already being provided.

In another example, however, a partnership seemed to have been strengthened by the fact that some member schools had formed a MAT, whilst some of the partners within this particular group belonged to other trusts. Interestingly, the chief executive of one of these trusts referred to the pressures she was under to expand her MAT. Despite this, she continued to have a significant role in the coordination of the area partnership.

Some partnerships had been successful in overcoming the difficulties created by school diversity. For example, a headteacher member of one partnership explained that it served a local authority that had *'one of everything'*. That is to say, in addition to maintained schools, there were selective schools, faith schools, single academies and MATs, and a range of specialist provisions. Despite this diversity, the partnership had been successful over many years in maintaining an inclusive stance.

Relationships with Local Authorities

Across the sample, there was a surprisingly mixed pattern in relation to this factor. Where relationships with senior officers were positive, this had helped to position partnerships as having a central role in strengthening local provision. On the other hand, we heard accounts of where breakdowns in these relationships had led those involved in coordinating partnerships to go through periods of uncertainty as to their future. In one case, frequent changes of local authority education directors had acted as a significant barrier to long-term planning.

In some instances, too, partnerships were seen as competing for 'business' with local authorities in relation to the provision of support, particularly regarding school improvement. Furthermore, our conversations with colleagues in various partnerships indicated that this is an area they are increasingly keen to lead on given the school-based expertise within their memberships.

The challenges and tensions associated with this matter were significant. Local authorities are still responsible for having oversight of all schools within their region, whereas these partnerships cannot necessarily guarantee, or may not even be set up to provide such coverage.

Availability of Resources

Predictably, those involved with the coordination of the partnerships saw resources as a constant challenge. Indeed, some expressed concern that their partnership could cease to exist in the near future because of the loss of funding from national government. Most of the partnerships in our sample involve schools in paying a membership fee or are planning to move towards this model.

In some instances, partnerships had recently been able to access resources from a local school support hub, although it was also noted that this was sometimes contingent on a willingness to focus on Government-driven priorities and recommended teaching practices. This is, of course, something of a distraction from the idea of locally defined improvement strategies determined by contextual analysis.

Lack of Mandate

A more subtle barrier related to the somewhat ambiguous status of the partnerships. This is not all bad news, however, in that it allows well-managed, local-coordinated partnerships that are relatively independent to occupy a crucial space in relation to the challenge of equity.

Where the partnerships had strong support from key partners, this allowed them to act quickly to address particular concerns. It is hardly surprising that, where this is seen to be effective, regional and national officials are willing to cooperate with locally led efforts in ways that strengthen their efforts.

That said, these school partnerships have no formal status that they can use to intervene where challenges exist. Providing a formal mandate to these structures, whilst at the same time allowing them discretion to act in relation to locally determined priorities, could be a major step forward in addressing the problems created by the current levels of fragmentation within local education systems in England.

Implications

The evidence of this small-scale study builds on the earlier report prepared by Christine Gilbert (2018) in which she argued that local area partnerships can provide the opportunity to *'shape a different model of professional accountability that motivates and inspires teachers, as well as incentivising system-wide collaboration'* (p. 6). With this in mind, by focusing on a relatively small sample, we were able to get closer to these eight partnerships in order to develop a greater understanding of what makes them work and the factors that inhibit their efforts.

In reflecting on these examples, it is important to acknowledge that they each remain fragile and imperfect, with their own limitations, difficulties, and risks. Moreover, it would be naive to underestimate the political complexities entailed. Much still depends on maintaining goodwill, sufficient stability and resourcing, and favourable inspection outcomes, among many other factors.

As far as we have been able to ascertain, the schools that make up the membership of the partnerships were involved of their own free will, because they saw a benefit to the young people and communities they serve. Despite what can be viewed as potentially unfavourable circumstances, the examples nonetheless indicate that professionals working in and around schools can influence local educational arrangements in order to make them more equitable. The evidence I have summarised also points to the sorts of conditions that are needed in order to use processes of collaboration between schools to foster equity within education systems. This is based on the idea that, in working together, schools can access untapped potential to improve their capacity for improving the achievement of all of their students, particularly those who are vulnerable to marginalisation or exclusion.

The challenge therefore is to mobilise this potential in order to develop a school-led strategy that works for all children and young people in a local area. This reminds us that educational improvement is, in essence, a social process that involves practitioners learning from one another, from their students, and from others involved in the lives of the young people they teach.

Peer Inquiry

Relevant to all of this, in various projects involving school partnerships, we have seen how the idea of peer inquiry can deepen relationships in positive ways. This approach involves the creation of groups of colleagues across a partnership of schools that work on solving real problems through cycles of inquiry and reflection. Trios of schools have proved to be a particularly effective way of using the approach.

The starting point for peer inquiry is the existing experience and knowledge of its members. Colleagues in the group are seen as sources of challenge and support, bringing their experiences and perspectives to the discussions that take place.

The suggested steps are as follows:

1 Representatives from the partner schools spend a morning together in each of their establishments, in order that the visitors can gather evidence about how improvement plans are being implemented. This might include discussions with a sample of staff and students, possibly through a series of 'learning walks'. It is suggested that the host school determines the exact focus for inquiry.

2 Towards the end of the morning the visitors meet to agree a list of thoughts regarding what has emerged. It is important to stress that these commentaries are not intended to be evaluative. Rather, they are a summary of interesting ideas that emerged during the visit.
3 The commentaries are intended to be used as the basis for discussion about the implementation of evidence-based improvement strategies within the host school. Later, they can also be used to stimulate discussion with other colleagues within the partner schools.

One of the most significant features of the visits carried out using peer inquiry is the way in which colleagues from different schools support one another in reviewing aspects of practice. We have found that these linking activities can shed new light on familiar situations, both for visitors and visited.

With this in mind, links between schools are made on the basis that the visitors are primarily there to assist the development of practices in the host school by generating evidence and reflecting together on the possible implications. In this way, visitors go both as colleagues and co-researchers, invited to find out more about the impact of existing practices.

Just to add, our experience suggests that researchers can sometimes make a useful contribution to such inquiry-based approaches to educational change (see examples in Ainscow, 2024a). Acting as consultants to partnerships as they seek to generate and engage with evidence, members of the research community can help to encourage an inquiring stance.

Looking to the Future

Reflecting on the evidence from the study of school partnerships reported in this chapter, my colleagues and I offered some suggestions on the possible implications for future policy and practice within the English education system. In particular, we considered what our findings mean in relation to the greatest challenge it faces, that of addressing equity.

It is important to recognise that current national policy in England, with its emphasis on school autonomy, competition, and choice, has injected new energy into the education system. In so doing, it has also provided incentives, encouragement, and the space for innovations of the sort that I have described to occur. At the same time, however, it has generated further barriers that are limiting the presence, participation, and achievement of some children and young people. It is also evident that these barriers are context specific. That is to say, they arise from the way that particular local education 'market places' privilege some learners at the expense of others. The implication is that there has to be some form of locally developed coordination and regulation.

Our proposal is that this could be achieved by the creation and strengthening of the sorts of area partnerships that I have described. However, for these partnerships to be effective, there needs to be strong political support for such a move, at both the national and local levels. Importantly, this must not involve the imposition of externally defined responses of the sort that have tended to be a feature of recent national initiatives in England. Rather, it should involve an organic process that is developed with respect for local circumstances.

Given current national policy in England, such an approach requires the mixing of an unusual cocktail of competition and cooperation, sometimes referred to as 'coopetition' (Muijs and Rumyantseva, 2014). This concept requires the following organisational conditions in order for it to be effective: partners who see clear and tangible benefits from collaboration; trust between partners, established through the careful development of relationships between key stakeholders; clear goals and agreements between partners; and forms of leadership that are skilful in managing tensions.

Informed by these ideas and the evidence that we generated through this particular study, my colleagues and I went on to argue that the development of school partnerships should be:

- Led locally by coordinating groups made up of experienced and credible practitioners;
- Underpinned by a clear purpose that both informs and drives decision-making and action;
- Autonomous in setting their own agenda;

- Evidence-based, leading to an analysis of the local context that identifies barriers experienced by some learners;
- Focused on finding ways of mobilising local expertise to address these barriers;
- Inclusive, in the sense that all schools and other centres of learning are involved, whatever their governance arrangements; and
- Linked to wider community resources.

All of this has important implications for the various key stakeholders within the education system. In particular, it requires teachers, especially those in senior positions, to see themselves as having a wider responsibility for all local children and young people, not just those that attend their own schools. For schools, this means aligning what they do with the efforts of other local players: not only partner schools but also employers, community groups, universities, public services, and so on.

It is also important to note that the more positive examples of schools collaborating involved shared leadership. In particular, we saw examples of headteachers working together and with other stakeholders to create a new form of middle tier. In these contexts, local authority staff were also seen to be taking on important new roles, facilitating these new arrangements and bringing to the discussions their wider knowledge of the local education system. Commenting on such 'leading from the middle' approaches in 2015, Andy Hargreaves and I argued that they can *provide a valuable focus for school improvement; be a means for efficient and effective use of research evidence and analysis of data across schools; provide support so schools can respond coherently to multiple external reform demands; and be champions for families and students, making sure everybody gets a fair deal*' (p. 44).

For local authorities, such developments mean adjusting their priorities and ways of working in response to improvement efforts that are led from within schools. At the same time, as I have suggested, their role must be to act as the 'conscience of the system', ensuring that all children and families are getting a fair deal. This is consistent with the view of Diane Reay (2022) who argues that radical changes are needed in order to promote equity within the English education system.

For her, it is the values and ethos that have to change, rather than expect any positive change to emanate from endless changes in policy.

Some Reflections

The study reported in this chapter offers reasons to be optimistic. Despite the highly competitive atmosphere that permeates the English education system and the fragmentation that this has encouraged, it is clear that there are many in the field whose instincts are to seek ways to work in partnerships. It is interesting, too, that many experienced school leaders, including some of those who manage MATs, are motivated to take on leadership roles that take them beyond their duties within their own institutions.

That said, although the examples we examined are fulfilling an important means of encouraging mutual support, there is much less evidence that they are making direct contributions to changes in practice that address the barriers faced by some learners. Where we saw evidence of this beginning to happen a common set of factors were in place. Most important of these was the use of available statistical data to identify worrying patterns in relation to factors such poor attendance, increased level of exclusions, and dips in outcomes as determined by results in test and examinations. What made these data more powerful, however, was when, as a result of the partnership structures, local practitioners were able to provide an informed interpretation to guide actions that were taken.

So, for example, in a few cases such processes pointed to responses that local authority staff could orchestrate in order to address worrying patterns. These responses might include more intensive school-to-school partnerships or additional support from another agency.

Other examples involved the generation of new data to investigate areas of growing concern. So, for example, a detailed investigation carried out by one partnership identified a significant increase in the numbers of children and young people being put forward for additional support, a trend that was putting enormous pressure on local authority funding. This led the partnership to work with local university staff in establishing an action research project to address this trend.

Examples such as these were not common across our eight cases. However, they illustrate the ways in which evidence-based interventions can be introduced into school partnerships in order to help strengthen equity within a local area.

Conclusion

The accounts presented in this chapter suggest that school-to-school collaboration can strengthen improvement processes by adding to the range of expertise made available. In particular, such arrangements have enormous potential for fostering the capacity of education systems to respond to learner diversity. More specifically, they can help to reduce the polarisation of schools, to the particular benefit of those students who are marginalised at the edges of the system, and whose progress and attitudes are a cause for concern. So, my fourth proposition is that *partnerships between schools should be developed in order to provide mutual challenge and support.*

However, we must be wary of falling into the trap of thinking all of this is simple and straightforward. For example, writing about the idea of school networking as an improvement strategy, Lima (2008) argues that, despite their growing prevalence, networks have become popular mainly because of faith and fads, rather than solid evidence of their benefits. There is, he argues, nothing inherently positive or negative about a network: '... *it can be flexible and organic, or rigid and bureaucratic; it can be liberating and empowering, or stifling and inhibiting; it can be democratic, but it may also be dominated by particular interests*' (p. 2).

6

BEYOND THE SCHOOL GATE

One of my roles as Chief Adviser for the Greater Manchester Challenge was to promote the initiative in the wider community. With this in mind, I visited many organisations in the city region to encourage them to get involved. So, for example, I spoke with representatives of the world-famous Hallé Orchestra, the four local universities, and the two major professional football clubs, as well as many smaller community groups.

Wherever I went the response was rather similar. Those involved talked about the many things they did with local schools but expressed frustration that they could do much more. The problem, they explained, is that folks in schools are so busy and have little time to discuss possible ways forward.

I relate this issue to research by my University of Manchester colleagues which suggests that the development of education systems that are effective for all children will only happen when what happens outside as well as inside a school changes (Kerr, Dyson and Raffo, 2014). Indeed, they provide encouraging evidence of what can happen when what schools do is aligned in a coherent strategy with the efforts of other community players – families, employers, community groups, universities, and public services. This does not necessarily mean schools doing more, but it does imply partnerships beyond the school, where partners multiply the impacts of each other's efforts. However, experience suggests that the success of such community partnerships is dependent upon a common understanding of what they are trying to achieve, an engagement with various forms of evidence to stimulate collective effort, and some form of local leadership.

Community Involvement

The approach I am suggesting builds on and widens the scope of the school partnerships discussed in Chapter 5. In so doing, it draws on the principles underpinning the highly acclaimed Harlem Children's Zone in the United States (Whitehurst and Croft, 2010). This involves efforts to improve outcomes for children and young people in areas of disadvantage through an approach that is characterised as being 'doubly holistic'. That is to say, it seeks to develop coordinated efforts to tackle the factors that disadvantage children and enhance the factors which support them, across all aspects of their lives, and across their life spans, from conception through to adulthood. Dobbie and Fryer (2009) describe the Children's Zone as *'arguably the most ambitious social experiment to alleviate poverty of our time'* (p. 1).

Another American initiative, StriveTogether, acts as a central backbone organisation for sites using similar ideas that are locally tailored (Grossman, Lombard and Fisher, 2014). These initiatives are guided by indicators that span young people's lives 'from cradle to career', with progress determined using data at all stages. The challenges involved in applying this thinking have also been explored in the Children's Neighbourhoods Scotland initiative (Drever, McLean and Lowden, 2021). And, currently, my colleagues and I are evaluating 'Cradle to Career', an ambitious initiative that seeks to raise the aspirations and improve the life-chances of all children and young people in North Birkenhead, a highly disadvantaged district in the North West of England.

Commenting on all of this, some of my University of Manchester colleagues have argued that attempts to create such place-based initiatives should not simply imitate what has happened in the United States (Dyson et al., 2013). Rather, they should seek to embody the principles that guide these developments but in ways that match the conditions in particular contexts. This means:

- Bringing together a range of partners;
- Creating a governance structure that gives them the degree of autonomy needed to act locally;
- Drawing funding and resources into these areas;

- Analysing how disadvantage 'works' in a local area;
- Formulating a strategic plan for tackling disadvantage across the childhood years and all the contexts in which children learn and develop; and
- Developing robust evaluation strategies to find out what works locally.

Such efforts can be led by any organisation or individual working on behalf of children and families. District staff may be key facilitators but do not necessarily have to be in the lead. Schools are essential partners, and headteachers – particularly when they represent groups of schools – are likely to be well placed to contribute to the leadership of such developments.

Although such place-based initiatives are sometimes used by policymakers as a vehicle to improve outcomes, they often fail to engage meaningfully with local resources. With this in mind, my colleagues have explored the idea of 'asset-based' approaches (Forbes and Kerr, 2021). These seek to understand how existing resources in disadvantaged places might contribute to improvement efforts. In particular, they stress the importance of working in partnership with young people (Forbes, 2022).

An inspiring example of how this thinking can be implemented is provided by Lingard et al. (2021), who developed the idea of 'learning commissions' to co-produce knowledge about community expectations of schools in Queensland, Australia. Their approach suggests a different approach to accountability than the more usual top-down approach based on testing. Rather, it places particular emphasis on listening to the voices of community members, particularly those who have previously been silenced, in order to improve learning outcomes for all young people.

The Impact of Market Forces

Returning to a theme running through this book, how feasible are such community-focused arrangements within those education systems where market forces are being used to foster system reform? These countries have set out with the dual aims of 'raising standards' overall, while also narrowing gaps between the most and least advantaged learners. In so doing, they have assumed that increased competition can provide schools with the freedoms and incentives needed to ensure that all learners succeed, regardless of their backgrounds.

In practice, this has resulted in a combination of measures to increase competition between schools (Au, 2009), free schools from local government management arrangements (Adonis, 2012), and hold school publicly to account on narrowly defined and attainment-focused measures of effectiveness (Schildkamp, Ehren and Lai, 2012). The introduction of charter schools in the United States, independent public schools in parts of Australia, free schools in Sweden, the voucher systems in Chile and, of course, academies in England, are all examples of this international direction of travel.

Having analysed this international movement, we have argued that the approach involves the following overall features (Salokangas and Ainscow, 2017):

- **Making schools more autonomous**. The logic is that giving schools more freedom will put them in a better position to address the needs of their students. In this way, it is assumed, more decisions can be made locally, by the people involved in the schools, rather than by administrators at the district level. The matters over which schools became more autonomous vary from one country to another but include, for example, increased decision-making capacity over curriculum, teaching practices, finance, and regulations concerning staff recruitment and contracts.
- **Bringing new 'actors' into the management, administration, and governance of schools**. The criteria concerning who these actors are varies from country to country. They may include organisations and individuals who have not traditionally been involved in the management of publicly funded education, such as private, semi-private and charitable organisations, parent groups, religious organisations, and wealthy philanthropists. These new contributors, it is argued, will bring fresh ideas that will inject new energy and more efficient ways of working into public education.
- **Introducing (or maintaining) heavily regulated quality assurance systems**. For example, in England, students enrolled

in academies sit the same national tests as those in other state schools and are subject to similar school inspections as others. The results of both the testing and the inspections are made publicly available. Such narrowly defined measures of effectiveness are used for accountability purposes, not only in autonomous schools but widely in the education systems.

The potential merits of this global trend towards marketisation remain a matter of considerable debate and there have been varied views as to its impacts. Reviewing the available international evidence, Muijs and Rumyantseva (2014) conclude that competition between schools *'leads to modest improvements in pupil attainment, but also to modest increases in socioeconomic and ethnic segregation'* (p. 3). Whilst this is in some ways encouraging, it is important to note that subsequent evidence from a range of countries has underlined concerns about segregation (see, for instance, Hatch et al., 2019; Hutchinson et al., 2020; Pickett and Vanderbloemen, 2015; Salokangas and Ainscow, 2017), with Michael Fullan (2021, p. 4) going so far as to argue that marketised systems have become 'catastrophically ineffective' in addressing inequalities and that nothing short of a 'radical paradigm shift' will change this situation.

Addressing the Challenges

This international trend points to one of the most pressing educational challenges of our time. On the one hand, there is good reason to believe that education systems working on market principles are failing to reduce inequalities and will continue to do so. Yet on the other hand, the political and economic capital invested in marketised arrangements is now so great that there is likely to be little political will to fundamentally disrupt or dismantle them. Even in Nordic countries that have historically operated on more collectivist principles - and enjoyed high attainments and relatively narrow gaps - market principles have become increasingly dominant, despite the resulting growth in inequalities (Safstrom and Mansson, 2022; Tervasmäki, Okkolin and Kauppinen 2020).

These trends point to a challenging question: *'how can greater equity be promoted within education systems based on market forces?'* With my colleagues, I have set out to address this matter from an applied, empirical stance. That is to say, we are concerned with the possibility of engaging community partners in supporting efforts to improve outcomes, particularly in high-poverty contexts.

My colleagues and I have long argued that, in these respects, some of the most valuable knowledge available about how to move marketised education systems in more equitable directions is likely to come from within these systems, and specifically from those working directly in and around schools serving high-poverty populations in high-poverty places (e.g., Ainscow, Chapman and Hadfield, 2020; Kerr, Dyson and Raffo, 2014). We also know from experience that, while these local professionals can be expert in finding opportunities to do things differently, their efforts are rarely visible beyond their immediate local contexts, meaning there is little opportunity to learn from them. Research therefore has a vital role to play in identifying and drawing out relevant lessons from places where local system arrangements are being remodelled gradually *from the bottom-up* to promote greater equity, and where these new arrangements are being sustained and are beginning to demonstrate impacts, however modest.

With a focus once again on England as an extreme case of the application of market principles, in what follows I explore the implications of this thinking, focusing in particular on ways of mobilising community resources. I begin by explaining some of the main challenges to equity in the current English context, before presenting some responses to these, as identified through our own research. I argue that these suggest ways of working that have the potential to promote greater equity.

The Context

As I have explained, in the last 30 years, England has seen the development of a market-driven approach to educational policies. These reforms have included the introduction of a national curriculum, coupled with centralised mechanisms to hold schools publicly to account. This has included the creation of public 'league tables' based on schools' performances in national-level standardised attainment tests. New forms of centrally managed school inspection have also been introduced, with punitive measures applied to those deemed 'underperforming' – from changes in school leadership, to school closure in extreme cases. All of this has resulted in the increased scrutiny of schools. It has also served to reinforce a narrow understanding of what counts as valuable educational outcomes, leading to a government preoccupation with identifying interventions that 'work' to improve attainment outcomes rapidly and at scale (Pampaka et al., 2016).

England has also promoted school autonomy as being central to its reforms, perhaps more intensively than any other country, primarily through its academies programme. Academies are state-funded schools that remain subject to regular inspection but sit outside local government control. Instead, they operate as self-governing, not-for-profit charitable trusts, with some additional freedoms from the national curriculum and national agreements on teachers' pay and conditions (Salokangas and Ainscow, 2017).

As originally conceived, academies were intended to replace inner-city secondary schools (for ages 11–16) judged as underperforming and requiring significant improvement. Since 2010, however, this focus has shifted to encouraging all schools to become academies.

Over the last decade, the pace of academisation has been fierce, with Ladd and Fiske (2016) dubbing England as the 'wild west' of academy reforms. While there were just 272 academies in England in the 2010–2011 academic year, by January 2023 40.4% of primary schools were academies, accounting for 42.1% of the primary school population, and 80.4% of secondary schools were academies, accounting for 80.2% of secondary school students (Kerr and Ainscow, 2023).

As academy numbers have grown, government has also encouraged the creation of multi-academy trusts (MATs). These are groups of academies with shared governance arrangements. Schools with poor performance on national measures have been pressured to join MATs on the assumption that relationships with higher-performing schools will support their improvement, with MAT-level performance league tables also being published by central government.

Emerging MAT arrangements have proved highly diverse, with a wide range of players who have differing motivations, expertise, and understandings of education and managing schools. For instance, while some MATs are locality-based, others operate nationally. Some are school-led, while others, led by church authorities, are exclusively for faith schools. There are others led by organisations with strong social responsibility remits but which may have little experience of managing schools, ranging, for example, from universities to registered social local landlords. Meanwhile, some are led by non-profit organisations created specifically to form MATs with the capacity to manage large numbers of geographically dispersed schools.

The rapid growth of academies has been matched by the increasing emasculation of local authorities with regard to educational arrangements. To give an example, following a day conference at which I spoke to all the headteachers in one local authority, I wrote the following note for my colleagues:

> Working mainly in areas where at least something is happening I had forgotten how bad things are when the current policies hit contexts that are struggling. In the case of this particular local authority, almost all the schools are academies and there are few contacts between the MATs that exist. Results are disastrously low, and there are large numbers of kids excluded or placed in alternative provision. A significant number of schools are in Ofsted categories.
>
> During the conference the headteachers of the handful of local authority maintained primary schools chose to sit together on a separate table, as did the group of LA officers.
>
> It seems to me that the only feasible way forward in such contexts are the sorts of areas partnerships that we are studying. But, how can this idea be introduced in a context like this one that is so massively fragmented?

Historically, the management of the English school system has relied on local authorities working with all the schools across an administrative area, with their roles including: arranging school admissions, supporting school improvement, and providing specialist services both directly to schools – from educational psychology and behaviour support, to administrative and financial functions – and through social care and welfare support for children and families, commonly referred to as 'children's services'.

However imperfect these arrangements may have been, they positioned local authorities to address wide-ranging inequalities at multiple levels – with individual children, families and schools, and at strategic area-levels. Now, however, local authorities are just one of a number of organisations managing the schools in an administrative area and have little direct influence over academies and MATs. In addition, austerity measures over the last decade have severely depleted the abilities of local authorities to provide specialist support services.

Impacts

There is much evidence to suggest that, although there have been positive impacts, these shifts in policy have had perverse effects for the most economically disadvantaged children and young people, and for the schools that serve them. Having previously been sustainable, over the last few years attainment gaps between the most and least advantaged students have begun to grow noticeably at both the primary and secondary levels (Elliott Major and Briant, 2023; Hutchinson et al., 2020). There have also been increasing reports of schools serving high-poverty contexts struggling to provide both basic welfare and more specialist health and social care services and without the funding, capacity, or expertise needed to do so (Reay, 2022).

Furthermore, as the school system has increasingly fragmented, some school leaders have become expert at 'protecting' their own schools by intentionally recruiting more advantaged student cohorts. For example, an independent commission into the implications of academy expansion reported that some academies were using their freedoms over admissions effectively to exclude children from poorer backgrounds by intentionally making the local authority's application forms inaccessible to some parents (Husbands et al., 2013).

Another concern has been the emergence of 'off-rolling' – defined as 'when a child is removed from the school roll for the school's benefit, rather than in the child's best interests' (Ofsted 2019). Meanwhile, a study reported that while behaviour was widely cited as the reason for removing a child from school, *'most teachers feel confident in agreeing that off-rolling is done to fix statistics for the benefit of the school in high stakes attainment tests*' (YouGov, 2019, p. 8). This research also found that vulnerable students were perceived to be disproportionately affected and were at risk of becoming trapped outside the school system, as local authorities were often unaware that they were not in school and had limited influence to arrange new school places.

Poorly performing schools within MATs have been affected by similar practices. For example, there have been instances of schools serving intensely disadvantaged populations that have been pressured to become academies and join a MAT and then removed from their MAT as a result of continuing poor performance. Mansell (2017) has termed these 'orphan' schools – cut off from their local authorities and unable to find other MATs to join. Indeed, a recent government report concluded that the *Department for Education… has not set out a clear policy for how it will ensure that trusts are being set up to best support pupils' and local need*' (Committee of Public Accounts, 2022), and there have also been reports of dubious financial practices in some MATs.

While this picture of the current context is far from comprehensive, it nonetheless serves to show that the English case is an extreme example of a growing international direction of travel. This also makes it an important case for the purposes of the argument developed in this book. If, as I will illustrate, there are still spaces within current arrangements in England where local practitioners can begin to remodel some aspects of the system on more equitable lines, it seems likely that similar, and perhaps greater, opportunities will exist in other marketised systems.

With this in mind, I turn now to outline the nature of the engagement my colleagues and I have had with emerging local area developments, before presenting examples, each of which demonstrates a different source of leadership for such reforms.

Analysing Developments

The examples I present are drawn from a 15-year research programme focused on equity within the English education system (see: Kerr and Ainscow, 2022). This was underpinned by a series of evidence-based processes, designed to support equitable developments in the field.

These assume that efforts to promote greater equity within a local area – and therefore the research that supports them – must:

- Seek to surface and challenge taken-for-granted assumptions about how education systems should operate;
- Focus specifically on the poorest learners and the schools that serve them;
- Value different forms of knowledge and expertise held by multiple, and often unheard, professional and community stakeholders;
- Intentionally move this knowledge and expertise around within and across systems to enhance learning about possibilities for more equitable practices;
- Support forms of collaborative action that seek to use such knowledge and expertise to stimulate more equitable practices; and
- Build the capacity of local stakeholders to develop and sustain collaborative action.

Often, we have been commissioned by emerging initiatives to support them in realising these principles. In doing so, we have sometimes employed a design-based implementation research methodology (Anderson and Shutack, 2012; Fishman et al., 2013).

Through this work we have developed a distinctive form of this approach, which we term 'design-based equity research' (Kerr and Ainscow, 2023). In summary, we see this as a principled approach broadly characterised by:

- A values framework which facilitates discussion of equity;
- The use of evidence (locally generated and from existing research) to drive change;
- A process of synthesis, accommodation, and mediation between different stakeholders' knowledge and perspectives (e.g., practitioners, policy-makers, researchers, students, parents, and community groups); and
- A strong iterative relationship between the values of equity, research evidence, and the process of intervening in local education systems, with values emerging, being refined, and given meaning in context.

Over time, we have come to understand the process of acting on these principles as fundamentally one of knowledge generation, in which practitioner and researcher expertise meet in particular contexts to produce new ways in which broad values of equity might be better realised in future practice. This has included developing the use of a theory of change approach that makes equity central to thinking about how interventions will work. Thus, whilst our approach owes much to established action-oriented approaches, these emphases, we believe, make a distinctive contribution to the wider field.

For our purposes, this approach has four important characteristics. Firstly, it assumes that the contexts where an intervention operates – in much of our research, high-poverty places – are integral to its design. Secondly, it treats interventions as being dynamic, assuming that they will develop over time through taking action. Thirdly, it involves intervention leaders and researchers working in partnership, and bringing their collective expertise and critical scrutiny to bear on developments. Fourthly, these practitioner-researcher partnerships support an iterative process of moving back and forth between context-specific and more general concerns. This can both strengthen local interventions by drawing on wider knowledge, while also supporting the development of transferable theories from local practices.

Operationally, we have employed a wide range of qualitative and quantitative methods, as suited to project requirements, and worked with diverse stakeholder groups, sometimes training them as co-researchers to lead research activities locally. Our engagement with local developments has also tended to be long-term, often with an initial period of quite intense research activity over a six-month to two-year period, which has then been sustained through ongoing 'light touch' engagements over a number of years. This prolonged engagement has enabled us to identify emerging bottom-up reform efforts that, while they inevitably remain works in progress, also show some evidence of sustainability and gains in equity.

Emerging Equitable Practices

In what follows I draw on work carried out in partnership with my University of Manchester colleague Kirstin Kerr in order to present three examples of efforts to develop area-based approaches to promote equitable educational arrangements emerging within high-poverty contexts in England. They indicate that leadership for such developments tends to come from one of three sources: schools working in more-or-less formal local alliances; local authorities seeking to redefine their relationships with schools; and third-sector organisations lying outside the education system but that are already working to address wider determinants of poor educational outcomes, for instance, in health or housing.

Local Alliances

As explained in the previous chapter, there is increasing evidence that collaboration between schools has potential for fostering system-wide improvement, not least in high-poverty contexts. This can be about transferring knowledge and expertise between schools, or by generating shared context-specific knowledge on which schools can act collectively.

We have worked in a variety of contexts where groups of schools within an area – whether defined administratively, or by the way people live locally – have developed such collaborative strategies to support their collective improvement. In some instances, these have focused most strongly on providing comprehensive pastoral and welfare supports. In others, as in the following example, they have maintained a tighter focus on improving attainment.

This example involves a local area-based partnership of 15 schools in the same local authority: 12 primary, 2 secondary and 1 special school, including a diverse mix of faith schools, academies, and maintained schools. Stimulated and strengthened at various times by government initiatives targeting high-poverty local authorities, the partnership has been maintained by participating schools in various forms for over 20 years, maintaining a focus on school improvement throughout. The schools all make an annual financial contribution to the running of the partnership, which covers the cost of employing a part-time partnership co-ordinator who manages its activities on a day-to-day basis.

The 15 headteachers meet monthly to make collective decisions about the partnership's offer, their stated aims being to:

- Secure the highest standards of teaching, learning, and achievement for all learners in the area;

- Improve opportunities for all learners and ensure the effective use of resources;
- Provide evaluation and challenge based on trust and reciprocity;
- Contribute to the professional development of all staff; and
- Disseminate good practice across the participating schools.

To realise these aims, the partnership developed a complex and continually evolving improvement model. For example, it worked with a leading national literacy charity and local library services to co-create a reading quality mark for its schools to follow which emphasises reading for enjoyment. It also created 'tripods' of primary schools, grouping these together by geographical proximity, with representatives from the partnership's two secondary schools also invited to join. Each tripod works on a particular improvement issue and then feeds back to the whole partnership, with this enhancing its knowledge and capacity to learn.

This example demonstrates that even when the schools serving a high-poverty context have different affiliations, local collaboration can still contribute to more equitable arrangements. These can include the pooling of resources for mutual benefit. The small-scale geographical nature of this particular partnership appears fundamental to its success. The partner schools all have a shared interest in the distinctive challenges and opportunities of the area they serve, which simply cannot exist in the same way in wider affiliations.

Redefining Relationships

While some local authorities have largely stepped back from managing educational arrangements, they nonetheless remain distinctively placed within the English education landscape. In particular, they have the potential to engage with a wider range of schools and services. Furthermore, unlike MATs, some of which have large numbers of schools in different parts of the country, they remain geographically anchored, with an understanding of local factors within their administrative boundaries.

Local authorities also still provide public services, however reduced, and not just to children and schools, but also in relation to housing, the environment, transport, leisure, business, and local democracy. This means that they are one of few organisations with the potential to engage with what Anyon (2005, p. 5) calls the *'educational policy panoply'*, i.e., the range of policies and services distal to, but nonetheless influential in, shaping and responding to educational inequities.

The following example illustrates how some English local authorities are seeking to capitalise on their distinctive position, using the breakdown of their historic roles as an opportunity to redefine their relationships with schools and remodel their services accordingly. It focuses on a district with approximately 150 primary schools and 50 secondary schools.

Schools serving the poorer communities have faced pressure to become academies, and while this seems to have worked well for some, others have been left feeling isolated and ill supported. Funding cuts have also considerably reduced the authority's capacity to provide specialist support services, and when schools have bought in external services, these have sometimes been of poor quality.

In response, this particular local authority has redefined its role, taking on three main functions. Firstly, it has positioned itself as a 'match-maker' between schools and the MATs they could potentially join. In particular, it actively seeks out trusts whose operating principles are well aligned with commitments to: (i) supporting schools to work together on an area-basis; and (ii) maintaining supportive relationships with local authority staff to ensure that schools are connected to wider service and policy developments in their administrative areas.

Secondly, all schools have been grouped into what are termed 'area-based hubs'. These are intended to serve as a platform for schools, services, and wider stakeholders to share local intelligence and develop collective strategies and actions in response. Practically, the hubs are led by local steering groups, including staff from schools, services, community organisations, and local residents.

Third, the local authority has developed strategies to reconfigure the services it offers to schools to ensure they reflect actual needs within the local hub-areas and are accountable to those they are designed to benefit. To this end, it has piloted the introduction of community-based accountability processes alongside statutory reporting requirements.

This example suggests that local authorities still have potentially important roles to play within the English education system. In particular, it indicates that they can help in creating new partnership arrangements for their own work with schools.

Third-sector Organisations

We have seen many examples suggesting that third-sector groups, such as charities, social enterprises, and community groups, can have important roles to play in addressing these issues. These may include non-profit organisations with expertise in providing particular kinds of services, for instance, specialist support for young people at risk of gang membership.

The following example is illustrative of this approach. It involved four schools (three primary, one secondary) serving a large social housing estate. It was initiated by experts from a national charity, in response to concerns about students' speech and language being far below age-related expectations. The charity supplied targeted and universal evidence-based interventions to foster language development, training teachers to use these and to understand typical development. It also brokered a relationship with a local clinical commission group to second a part-time National Health Service therapist to support teachers and parents in developing children's speech and language development.

The charity also supported schools in exploring what was happening in children's wider environments to contribute to delayed speech and language development. For example, through home visits and work with health visitors, the schools found that some young single mothers were being prioritised for housing in the area but often had to move away from their existing support networks, leaving them socially isolated. In addition, many parents lacked good levels of oracy and self-esteem, rarely left the estate, and were reluctant to engage with early years settings or local library services. This limited children's exposure to varied language contexts, parents' knowledge about how to support their child's development, and opportunities to build their confidence around this.

Drawing on the charity's expertise, the schools developed a raft of locally tailored responses, ranging from: exploring whether births could be registered in the local children's centre so all parents could be welcomed into the service; school-based stay and play sessions where parents and children made puppets together and parents learnt how to tell stories at home using the puppet, to develop their child's narrative skills; introducing KS3 subject specialist vocabulary into KS2 to aid transition; and exploring different models of peer mentoring to help overcome parental isolation.

Parents engaging in school-based activities were, in effect, training as mentors, with support from the schools, local health visitors, and children's centre, who were also working together to identify potential mentees. In under a year, the schools saw notable improvements in speech and language, higher levels of active engagement from targeted groups of parents, and new relationships and resource sharing amongst schools, and between schools and other agencies.

This example suggests that leadership for equitable educational development need not always come from within an education system. As we see, external organisations operating in high-poverty contexts can have the potential to encourage new approaches and enrich the system, bringing their additional expertise, knowledge and resources.

Drawing Out the Lessons

Reflecting on these examples it is important to acknowledge that each remains fragile and imperfect, with its own limitations, difficulties, and risks. Moreover, it would be naïve to underestimate the political complexities entailed. Much still depends on maintaining goodwill, sufficient stability and resourcing, and favourable inspection outcomes, among many other factors.

Despite these potentially unfavourable circumstances, the examples indicate that professionals working in and around schools can influence local educational arrangements in order to make them more equitable. Together they suggest that:

- Place-based school-to-school collaboration can better support improvement for all;

- This requires an emphasis on collective action, not just individual accountability;
- Local authorities can have important coordinating and quality assurance roles;
- In particular, authorities can help to counter some of the vagaries of opening service provision and school management to the market;
- Leadership for equitable developments need not always come from those directly engaged in schooling: some third sector organisations may be well-placed to do so and less constrained by education system arrangements; and
- Equitable reform efforts have to recognise the value of local professionals' knowledge of working in high-poverty contexts, and of university research that can help to surface this and enable its use.

Keeping this analysis in mind, I suggest that market-driven education systems must do more to recognise the importance of local contexts in shaping system arrangements. Whilst the introduction of market forces may have been widely seen as a means to break the link between education and disadvantage by allowing parents to choose schools outside their local areas, and in England, by enabling schools to join MATs with others from outside their locales, the link remains and cannot be ignored. Many children in high-poverty contexts will still attend schools in those contexts. Whatever their wider affiliations, schools serving those contexts will still need to address barriers to learning arising from children's home and community contexts. The third example suggests that even when children travel to schools outside their local neighbourhoods, the challenges they face remain, even if schools do not recognise them.

All of this suggests that equitable reforms must actively engage, both conceptually and pragmatically, with the challenges and opportunities presented by high-poverty contexts. Conceptually, an active engagement with places as they are 'lived' appears vital. Whatever tangible or measured characteristics high-poverty contexts share, they are also to some extent unique, continually being shaped and reshaped by the ways in which their geographical, physical, and service infrastructures, histories, cultures, and demographics, and the norms, networks, and behaviours of the people who live there, interact and change over time (Galster 2001). In addition, however austere the times, high-poverty contexts still hold resources that can support children's education – whether public or third-sector services operating locally, or other kinds of tangible and intangible assets (Forbes and Kerr 2021).

In a way that helps to draw these points together, Smith (1999) has argued that while some inequalities can only be addressed at the national government level, there are others that can only be understood and addressed at an area level, by local actors with a deep knowledge of the places where they work and who can access local resources. The examples I provide point to the power of education and local professionals acting on their local knowledge and harnessing local resources to develop co-ordinated and strategic actions. In doing so, they also diverge markedly from the approach recently pursued by the English government as part of what is calls its 'levelling up' strategy (HM Government 2022). As my colleague Kirstin Kerr argues, this treats high-poverty areas as 'containers' into which interventions that 'work' can be dropped, rather than as dynamic entities that present both challenges to, and opportunities for, equitable reforms.

Conclusion

Early on in this chapter, I posed the question *'how can greater equity be promoted within education systems based on market forces?'* The examples I have reported are to varying degrees fragile, localised, and inevitably limited in what they can achieve. Nonetheless, they point to how more equitable arrangements could be developed and the conditions needed to support this. They suggest that equitable systems must be connected, and that schools need to work together, and with other organisations, both within and beyond their local areas. They also point to the vital role of local collaborative activities in promoting greater equity, and the value of knowledge held by practitioners working in high-poverty contexts in informing these developments. They show, too, that pursuing more equitable arrangements does not always mean schools individually doing more, but it does imply partnerships beyond the school gate, where partners multiply the impacts of each other's efforts. These experiences lead to my fifth proposition: *families and other community partners should be encouraged to support the work of schools.*

As I have argued, the development of education systems that are effective for all children will only happen when what happens outside as well as inside a school changes. Indeed, there is encouraging evidence of what can happen when what schools do is aligned in a coherent strategy with the efforts of other community players – families, employers, community groups, universities, and public services. I argue that this does not necessarily mean schools doing more, but it does imply partnerships beyond the school, where partners multiply the impacts of each other's efforts.

There are significant implications here for national policy-makers. To promote greater equity, they need to develop 'intelligent' policy that can learn from and nurture innovative developments. They also have to determine how they can foster the conditions needed to encourage the interpretation of policy on the ground in ways that promote greater equity, rather than being manipulated for institutional gain. To inform this, it will be important to commission research that can identify, support and learn from emerging developments, without being unduly restricted by narrow concerns about 'what works'. Indeed, if Michael Fullan's call for a paradigm shift is to be realised, it will most likely be through finding and sharing learning from a growing number of 'anomalous developments' (Mills and Sacrez, 2020) that enact the principles proposed in this book.

7
PROVIDING SUPPORT AND CHALLENGE

Some years ago, I attended a meeting of local authority advisers in Greater Manchester as they debated their roles within what was a changing policy context. When the discussion became rather heated, one member of the group commented: *'Look colleagues, this is simple: the job of schools is to improve themselves. Our job is to make sure it happens'*.

In this chapter, I consider what it is that those at a local area level can contribute to efforts to promote inclusion and equity across an education system. I do this by reflecting further on my work within the government-instigated improvement initiatives described in Chapter 3: London Challenge, from 2002 to 2011; the Greater Manchester Challenge, from 2007 to 2011, and Schools Challenge Cymru, from 2014 to 2017. All of these projects involved teams of what were called challenge advisers and focused on finding ways of breaking the link between disadvantaged home backgrounds and educational outcomes.

Roles of the Middle Tier

The creation of a system for improvement that is driven by schools themselves, and that involves cooperation between schools and with other community organisations, begs questions regarding the roles of school districts. Indeed, it raises the possibility that the involvement of a middle-level administrative structure may not even be necessary.

The authors of the influential McKinsey report (Mourshed, Chijioke and Barber, 2010), having analysed *'how the world's most improved school systems keep getting better'*, express surprise at the critical role that what they call the 'mediating layer' plays between school delivery and central government This led them to conclude that sustaining system improvement in the longer term requires 'integration and intermediation' across each level of the system, 'from the classroom to the superintendent or minister's office'. They explain:

> The operating system of the mediating layer acts as the integrator and mediator between the classrooms and the centre. This is not to suggest that school reforms should begin here. In every system we looked at, the first focus of school reforms was on the schools and the centre. Efforts to strengthen the mediating layer usually came later, as the need for an active intermediary in delivering the system improvements became clearer.
>
> (p. 82)

The authors of the report go on to suggest that the specific functions the mediating layer plays are: providing targeted support to schools; acting as a buffer between the centre and the schools, while interpreting and communicating the improvement objectives in order to manage any resistance to change; and enhancing the collaborative exchange between schools, by facilitating the sharing of best practices, helping them to support each other, share learning, and standardise practices.

Writing about system reform in 2015, Andy Hargreaves and I argued for paying attention to the potential of district support for schools and teachers in innovating and improving together. With this in mind, we argued for the adoption of a 'leading from the middle' approach, in which *'districts don't just mediate and manage other people's reforms individually; they become the collective drivers of change and improvement together'* (p. 9).

Developing this theme in a recent book, Hargreaves (2023) argues that, for him, the middle is not 'a linkage' but 'a driving force': *'... a mover and shaker for policy and change towards more inclusive educational values'* (p. 7). Drawing on a ten-year period of research in ten of Ontario's 72 school districts, Hargreaves and his colleague (2020) conclude that such an approach:

> ... engages and empowers a strong profession to serve and support learning and well-being for all students within and across local and diverse communities.
>
> (p. 110)

Similarly, Michael Fullan (2015) describes leadership from the middle as:

> [...] a deliberate strategy that increases the capacity and internal coherence of the middle as it becomes a more effective partner upward to the state and downward to its schools and communities, in pursuit of greater system performance [...]. This approach is powerful because it mobilizes the middle (districts and/or networks of schools), thus developing widespread capacity.
>
> (p. 1)

Certainly, the experience of the Challenge programmes in the United Kingdom suggests that district staff have an important role to play, not least in making sure that all children and young people are getting a fair deal. In order to do this, they need to have the big picture about what is happening in their communities, identifying priorities for action and brokering collaboration. This is likely to involve significant structural and cultural changes, with local authorities moving away from a command and control perspective, solely focused within their own boundaries, towards one of enabling and facilitating collaborative action across borders.

However, in the system change initiatives I have described, local authority colleagues often found these changes challenging, particularly during times of reducing budgets. The strengthening of cross-border cooperation at many levels provided contexts within which mutual support could be provided in addressing these concerns. In this way, officers and support staff at the local area level were able to assist one another in addressing new policy demands.

Support Strategies

Within the Challenge programmes in London, Greater Manchester, and Wales, the aim was to 'get behind' people in schools, on the assumption that if they were to make progress they would improve themselves. Analysis of context was crucial in this respect, the purpose being to build on relative strengths within individual schools and address areas of their work that were a cause for concern. This led us to explore how advisers can provide effective ways of supporting change.

One source of information regarding support was provided through the 'families of schools' data system, in which schools within a region were grouped on the basis of the profiles of the communities they served (Ainscow, 2015). In this way, schools could compare their current levels of student achievement with those found in similar schools. And, in so doing, they could also locate schools with relevant strengths that they might choose to approach for support.

Meanwhile, as I explained in Chapter 3, those schools facing particular difficulties were designated as the 'Keys Success' and received more intensive support from a challenge adviser. Through their involvement in the process of assessing the context and formulating a plan of action, the advisers were then in a position to evaluate whether other, more drastic actions were needed in order to secure the school's improvement. And, of course, in some instances, this might mean a decision that the head, or other senior staff, did not have the capabilities to lead the process.

The approach used in those schools facing challenging circumstances was based on a detailed analysis of the local context and the development of an improvement strategy that fitted these circumstances. The challenge advisers had a central role here, working alongside senior school staff in carrying the analysis and mobilising external support where needed.

Keys to Success

Drawing on successful experiences in London, something like 200 schools took part for various periods in the Keys to Success process over the three years of the Greater Manchester Challenge. Initially, schools tended to be reluctant to join what was seen as a 'club for failing schools'. However, as success stories started to spread across the city region this began to change. Indeed, for some schools, the title Keys to Success became a badge of honour, with some signalling the fact on their websites and letterheads. Further impetus to all of this came about as word got around that some of these schools were now being invited to be the strong partner supporting other schools facing difficulties.

Admission to the programme resulted from a process of negotiations between challenge advisers and local authority officers. This was usually referred to as 'triage', a term used traditionally to describe the priority setting that occurs in relation to medical emergencies and disasters. Sometimes this led to disputes when those involved had different assessments of the situation in particular schools. As the challenge advisers got closer to the contexts, however, they were in a stronger position to judge the quality of recommendations made by their local authority colleagues.

In many cases, evidence from test and examination results, plus the outcomes of inspections, meant that the decision was relatively straightforward. Nevertheless, there were situations where there were warning signs that a school was in rapid decline, including some that had good reputations in their communities. Our concern was that some local authorities officers did not have sufficient knowledge of their schools to make such assessments.

The interventions in the Keys to Success schools were developed as result of a close analysis of existing practices that looked to determine why progress was not occurring, whilst at the same time locating examples of good practice to build on. The approach used in each school was unique – often referred to by the advisers as 'bespoke' – based on a detailed analysis of the local context and the development of an improvement strategy that fitted the circumstances. In general terms, the focus was usually on the sorts of factors mentioned in our earlier research: strengthening teaching and leadership practices, student tracking systems, and raising expectations amongst staff, students, and parents.

The challenge advisers had a central role here, working alongside senior school staff in carrying out the initial analysis and mobilising external support. In many instances, an accelerated improvement board was created which met regularly in order to ensure momentum was maintained. Usually, the membership of these boards consisted of the head, chair of governors, a local authority representative, and the challenge adviser.

Crossing Borders

It became increasingly apparent that much of the progress made in the Keys to Success schools was achieved through carefully matched pairings (and sometimes trios) of schools that cut across social 'boundaries' of various kinds, including those that separate schools that are in different local authorities. In this way, expertise that was previously trapped in particular contexts was made more widely available. This led the advisers to place increasing emphasis on this strategy. In so doing, they also refined their own skills in making the approach work, becoming, as I sometimes joked, a kind of dating agency for the city region. As we hoped, it also became clear that the progress that these schools made helped to trigger improvements across the system.

Crossing borders sometimes involved what seemed like unlikely partnerships, as reported in the Guardian newspaper.[1] For example, a highly successful primary school that caters for children from Jewish Orthodox families worked with an inner-city school – one of the largest in the city region – to develop more effective use of assessment data and boost the quality of teaching and learning. This school has a high percentage of Muslim children, many of who learn English as a second language. Over a period of 18 months, the partnership contributed to significant improvements, as reflected in test results. It also led to a series of activities around wider school issues, such as the creative arts and the use of student voice, where the two schools shared their expertise. The headteacher of the Jewish school commented:

> It's been a totally positive experience, built on mutual respect. This (the partner school) is a great school and the learning is definitely a two-way process.

Another unusual partnership involved a primary school that had developed considerable expertise in teaching children to read, supporting a secondary school in another local authority where low levels of literacy have acted as a barrier to student progress. Describing what happened, the head of the primary school commented:

> Together we have developed the use of a letters and sounds phonics strategy to support improvements in literacy among the three lowest English sets in Year 7, including students with special educational needs. We had seen real impact using a more multi-sensory approach to the teaching of phonics within in our own school and I couldn't see any reason why it shouldn't be used to similar effect with older students.

She went on to talk with enthusiasm about the professional development opportunities all of this had provided for her own staff. News of the success of this particular partnership was spread around the city region and soon there was a queue of secondary schools waiting for similar support.

A striking feature of the partnerships that were most effective was the sense of joint responsibility that developed between schools, such that there was a shared commitment for the success of one another. I was reminded of this when I was told the story of a Roman Catholic secondary school in a relatively privileged district that supported a poorly performing school in another authority, where many of the students came from economically poor homes. Apparently, on the day that the second school was being inspected, a senior member of staff in the partner school suggested to her headteacher that they should pray for their colleagues. Whilst I am not qualified to comment on the effectiveness of this approach, the good news was the inspection resulted in a positive report.

Supporting Improvements

The approach used by the challenge advisers in London, Greater Manchester and Wales to support the process of change varied from school to school. Nevertheless, there was an overall pattern that guided these interventions. This was helpfully summed up in a set of notes written by a challenge adviser, Andrew Morley. He wrote:

> The following is a brief reflection on the process I engage with while working as a challenge adviser. Whilst it is written as a linear process, in practice it was never like this. That said, I feel that the following is a

useful and authentic guide to what happened when working with challenging schools.

Step one: an initial review process using key documents and data. This involved working with local authority colleagues to carry out a review to ensure the right schools were targeted for involvement. Having identified schools, I carried out a further review, using statistical evidence, inspection reports, local authority and internal evaluations, to achieve an overview of the quality and effectiveness of individual schools.

Step two: establish a framework for the improvement process. This involved me in working with the leadership of each school in carrying out an inquiry in order to establish improvement targets, proposed actions, intended outcomes and a timescale for completion. This was supported by systematic quality assurance to ensure standards were being achieved and accountability was real. Due to the nature and speed of change, this was a constant and cyclical activity within the improvement drive.

Step three: implement activities to impact on the priority areas. Whilst the targets for most schools tended to fall within the areas of leadership, learning, teaching and community links, there was a drive to ensure they were relevant to the particular context and tightly focused. In response to these targets, working with colleagues was crucial, such as colleagues from within the Challenge team and the local authority, in deciding what the support package should be for each school and when it should be deployed.

Step four. Support, challenge and manage the development of improvement activities. This was crucial to ensure that: the change process was being managed effectively; each school turned its plan into actions, making and consolidating progress as appropriate; there was systematic monitoring of the impact of all aspects of the support package and the contributions of stakeholders; and there was effective monitoring of school performance to ensure targets were being achieved.

Step five: Effective reporting procedures. These were intended to ensure that stakeholders were informed of all aspects of progress at the individual and authority level. As part of my routine work, after each school visit I completed a 'note of visit', which highlighted progress with specific reference to: the quality of school self-evaluation; progress on achieving priorities in the school's improvement plan; impact of the support package; key competence issues and issues for celebration; and recommendations for the next phase of improvement.

Occasionally the situation within a school was such that it was felt necessary to establish what we termed as an 'accelerated improvement board', to be convened and chaired by the headteacher. The other members of this board were the chair of governors, a representative of the local authority, a headteacher from a local cluster school, and the challenge adviser. The main task of these boards, which would meet monthly, was to ensure that the improvement strategies were being implemented effectively and that rapid progress was being made.

In a few instances, it was found that the headteacher did not have the confidence and skills necessary to act as the chair. Where this was the case the challenge adviser took on the role in an effort to model what was required. With coaching, the head would eventually take over. Such experiences illustrate the sensitive contexts in which advisers are sometimes required to work.

Team Work

Our earlier research underlined the importance of advisers operating as a team (Ainscow, Howes and Tweddle, 2006). With this in mind, the challenge teams met together on a regular basis to support one another's work. Whilst the content of these meetings varied, there were usually two core agenda items: firstly, a briefing regarding overall developments, including updates of policy changes from central Government; and secondly, what was called the 'professional hour', during which members of the team debated the challenges they faced generally, and in respect to particular schools or local authorities. These discussions proved to be tremendous opportunities for collective learning, as these teams of highly experienced professionals argued about what actions should be taken. For me personally, it was a privilege to sit back and reflect on the ideas that were generated by these groups of practitioners.

In some instances, the challenges presented by certain Keys to Success schools meant that they would occasionally be revisited during team meetings in order to hear about what progress, if any, was being made. For example, a primary school where overall standards were low in terms of attendance and results on national tests, and where there were also concerns about poor behaviour amongst pupils, was a regular focus of attention. The school had had a succession of headteachers, most of whom had stayed around for relatively short periods. Meanwhile, confidence amongst staff had declined and there were regular disputes amongst staff and school governors, which led to the involvement of teacher unions.

Over a period of two years, the challenge adviser assigned to this particular school gradually got to grips with the situation, with support from other members of the team. Interestingly, some years later I heard that the school had been graded 'outstanding' as a result of an inspection.

Addressing Obstacles

It is clear that these types of intervention require some form of locally led coordination in order to determine needs, engage stakeholders, and broker partnerships. The successful examples of this that we found suggest a possible way forward. They involve shared leadership from within schools, built on previous experiences of schools collaborating that had helped to develop relationships and confidence in sharing responsibility. However, our research led to what was, for me, a surprise in respect to the significant roles played by advisory staff. In some contexts, their actions acted as obstacles to local cooperation, whereas elsewhere they made crucial contributions to its success. This relates to the work of Louis (2013), who notes that district-managed networks in contexts of high accountability can sometimes generate high levels of fear and undermine efforts to shift responsibility for accountability to network leaders.

In what follows I look more closely at what all of this may involve by drawing on other recent experiences of trying to foster place-based partnerships using the thinking developed as a result of the initiatives described earlier in this chapter. The difficulties the two contexts faced related to geographical and historical factors. In recent years, however, these have been compounded by pressures created by the greater emphasis on competition and choice that has been introduced by the English national policy for education described in the previous chapter, not least the move towards school autonomy in the form of academies.

A Divided City

The first context is a city in the south of England that is divided on socio-economic grounds: on one side of the city there is a high concentration of low-income families, whilst relatively better off families are mainly on the other side. The school system largely reflects this sense of social division, particularly at the secondary phase.

Amongst the secondary schools, there are a few grammar schools, which select their students at the age of 11 based on performance in tests. The other secondary schools usually reflect the local communities in which they are located. Consequently, students from relatively disadvantaged backgrounds tend to be concentrated in particular schools. As a result, the city has what can be seen as a 'pecking order' of schools, from some that are highly regarded through to others that are much less popular.

The city's education system has been a cause for concern for some years, particularly its secondary schools where overall standards, as determined by scores on GCSE examinations and inspections, are relatively low. Following the election of the Conservative-led coalition in 2010, a series of strategies led the profile of its secondary schools to be transformed, such that there are now maintained schools, academies, special schools, grammar schools, a studio school, a university technology school, and special schools, plus a number of alternative provisions for excluded students. In this sense, the city is a relatively extreme version of the pattern that has been developing across the country

The story goes that, following an event in 2011 at which a senior government official spoke, many of the secondary schools in the city rushed to convert to academy status. Gradually, these were assimilated into various MATs, usually following a period of difficulty. As a result, the system became exceptionally fragmented, with a significant proportion of schools seen as underperforming. Most of these are concentrated in the area of the city that serves disadvantaged communities. A few are in crisis, with uncertainties as to their future existence. At the same time, in recent years student exclusions have increased, with the pupil referral unit, which is also an academy, appearing to want to expand its numbers.

This apparent crisis led to a decision in early 2018 by officials from the local authority and the office of the regional school commissioner to instigate its own City Challenge. I was invited to chair the first year of the project, which was launched at a conference of head teachers and senior staff from the various multi-academy trusts involved in the city. After this event, the decision was made that the initial focus should be on the secondary sector, where there was most concern about levels of achievement.

Following the patterns of our earlier projects, particularly, the Central South Wales Challenge (described in Chapter 3), a strategy group was formed made up of a group of headteachers, which I chaired. Meetings of the group were also attended by officers from the regional school commission and one from the local authority.

The discussions, which were informed by the ideas presented in the earlier chapters of this book, led to the production of a discussion paper to be shared with other stakeholders. In the paper, it was argued that the guiding vision would be of a high-performing system at the forefront of developments to find more effective ways of breaking the link between poverty, low attainment, and limited life chances. Central to this vision was the idea of a self-improving system – driven by school leaders and involving practitioners at all levels – that takes collective responsibility for the quality of education across the city.

It was noted in the discussion paper that it would be vital to involve other stakeholders, including local businesses, higher education institutes, health and social care professionals, sports and arts organisations, religious groups, and the voluntary sector. Informed again by my earlier experiences, this was seen as a recognition that closing the gap in outcomes between those from more and less advantaged backgrounds would only happen when the experience of children outside as well as inside school changes.

Initial discussions within the strategy group emphasised that the project must 'go beyond talk'. It was also recognised that it should not replicate existing initiatives and coordinating arrangements, although these would be built on and, where necessary, strengthened. Rather, it would seek to make a distinctive contribution, adding value to the work that was already going on.

The overall focus would be on the challenges associated with equity across the city, recognising that whilst the system works well for many young people, there is a significant proportion that is left behind. It was noted that many of these young people were at risk of cycles of unemployment, with long-term scarring effects for them as individuals, their families, and the wider community. In this respect, it was concluded that doing more of the same – however well – was unlikely to make a difference to this minority of young people.

The intention was to have a long-term sustainable impact on the way that the education system does its business. However, the strategy group believed that it was necessary to focus on certain immediate concerns and opportunities in order to kick-start the process of change. Broadly stated, the initial focus of activities was concerned with ensuring that all young people in the city would have:

- The best start in life, such that they grow up inspired to exceed expectations;
- Access to a suitably varied range of learning pathways; and
- The life skills they will need for the future, as well as the academic and technical qualifications to succeed.

In addressing this agenda, the strategy group planned to take on the following roles:

- **Contextual analysis** – This would involve having the 'big picture' regarding the current situation, in order to determine barriers that are preventing the progress of some learners and the resources that can be mobilised in order to overcome these barriers. It therefore required an analysis of the best available evidence regarding the progress of young people through education and training across the city.

- **Coordination** – This meant ensuring that schools that are experiencing particular difficulties have access to effective forms of support. It would also involve finding effective ways of joining up services and provisions to support and enhance the progress of the most vulnerable groups of learners, including those with special needs. In addition, it would involve providing support for the implementation of externally funded improvement initiatives in order that they have maximum reach and impact.
- **Collaboration** – The aim was to engage partners – within the city and beyond – in working together to move the system forward with pace. In so doing, it was seen to be essential to ensure that schools do not collude with one another to reinforce mediocrity and low expectations. Efforts would also be made to strengthen links with employers and higher education institutions in order to broaden curriculum opportunities and ensure that all young people are informed about career opportunities available in the labour market, as well as equipping them with high levels of resilience.
- **Promotion** – The Challenge 'brand' opened up new possibilities for the creation of an image of the city as an excellent place to live, learn and work. At the same time, there was a need to promote the city as a centre of creativity and innovation in relation to educational equity, such that it will be attractive to well-qualified, ambitious practitioners. With this in mind, efforts would also be made to ensure that there are high-quality opportunities for professional development.

As we see, the approach outlined in the discussion paper was based on ideas that had emerged from the initiatives described in earlier chapters, in particular, the belief that education systems have untapped potential to improve their capacity for improving the achievement of all young people. The aim, therefore, was to mobilise this potential. This reinforced the argument that educational improvement is a social process that involves practitioners in learning from one another, from their students, and from others involved in the lives of the young people they teach. An engagement with evidence was seen as a powerful catalyst for making this happen.

In moving forward, the strategy group recognised that it would be important to adopt an inclusive approach that draws stakeholders together to shape, implement and evaluate any changes that are introduced. In this context, differences – amongst students, teachers, schools, and communities – were seen to be a positive source of stimulation that could encourage new thinking and practices in order to engage hard-to-reach learners. However, this needed to be developed into a clear set of actions and structures that would galvanise the potential of the city.

As this process of planning developed, continuing discussions were going on in the background with local authority and regional government staff regarding their roles. Some contact was also made with local politicians. These discussions involved a constant struggle to convince these colleagues that, although they had important roles to play, decisions regarding the strategy had to be made by the group of headteachers. At the same time, many of the headteachers expressed informal doubts as to the degree of authority they had been given in a way that echoed my experiences in Central South Wales. Further doubts regarding all of this related to the availability of additional funding, which had been provided initially by regional government.

At a meeting in June 2018 of all the secondary heads, plus senior staff from the various multi-academy trusts, representatives of the strategy group presented the approach they were proposing for the following school year. It was evident that this was well received and the meeting concluded with what appeared to be a consensus that the recommended strategy should be taken forward.

Gradually, however, over the following year, it became evident that momentum had been lost. The headteacher strategy group stopped meeting, with the initiative becoming just another item on the agenda of occasional meetings of all the secondary heads in the city.

The sense of different players looking for somebody else to blame was reflected in an article that appeared in a local newspaper. In it, the regional director of the national inspection agency, Ofsted, was quoted as saying that school and political leaders across the city needed to make more effort. He suggested that *parents also need to pull up their socks, with unacceptable numbers of children turning up for their first day at primary school unready to learn. Many are not even toilet-trained by the time they arrive in class'*. He then urged parents: *'Put your smartphones down and talk to your children'*.

It is worth adding that I was told recently by a senior education officer in the region that there is evidence that this Challenge initiative did kick-start a longer-term process that has subsequently led to significant improvements across the city's schools. This reminds us, yet gain, that significant reform takes time to have an impact.

Collaboration Can Be a Barrier

This second example arises from the work of an Education Commission set up in 2016 in a small local authority in the north of England. I was member of the group set up to guide its work.

The local community is predominantly white and there are high levels of poverty. Over many years, the area and its education system have been subject to massive negative publicity nationally. The Education Commission was established to drive improved educational outcomes across the borough, building on best practice and providing challenges where needed to address the underlying causes of educational underperformance in local schools. I was a member of the Commission, the meetings of which were attended by senior officers from the local authority and the regional schools commissioner.

Over a two-year period, the Commission carried out a series of initiatives to support local stakeholders in working together to strengthen the education system. Whilst the impact of some of these was disappointing, they all helped to throw light on the barriers that have previously prevented the progress of some learners. At the same time, they identified what looked to be promising pathways for the future.

So, for example, it became clear that the local authority faced particular challenges in relation to the strengthening of its school system. These related, in part, to factors in the wider community, not least the high levels of economic disadvantage that exist. There were also historical factors that seemed to have created an atmosphere of low expectations that pervaded the school system, particularly at the secondary level. Here, the exodus of large numbers of young people to schools outside of the authority at the age of 11 has a major impact on what happens. If that was not enough of a problem, some of these students return at a later stage as a result of their being excluded from their schools because of low attainment and/or bad behaviour.

The long-term impact of local and national media attention on the low levels of performance in examinations, plus the legacy of well-intentioned external interventions that had not made a significant difference, had reinforced a widely held feeling in the area that little else can be done to bring about significant change. This was reflected in a tendency for colleagues within the schools to argue that 'we have tried that' to any suggestions made. There was also evidence of an inward-looking emphasis, a feature that may have resulted from factors such as the size of the authority, the lack of effective regional leadership, and negative reactions to a sense of being continually under the spotlight. In addition, some schools had a dependent relationship with the local authority, whilst at the same time blaming it for the lack of progress.

Nevertheless, there were positive features that could be built upon. In particular, there was a strong loyalty to the local authority 'brand', as evidenced by the continued involvement of senior school staff in meetings and events organised by the local authority. There were also resources in the local area that could be mobilised, not least through the contributions of school governors. In addition, the continuing commitment to three long-established area collaboratives was evidence of a sense of 'togetherness', particularly in the primary sector.

The Commission had some success in getting the three collaboratives to learn from one another. However, despite this progress, the work of these groupings appeared to remain largely at a superficial level, with schools taking part in their activities but unwilling to explore deeper forms of cooperation that would involve a much greater emphasis on mutual challenge. The programmes of the collaboratives also continued to take the form of rather traditional conferences and workshops that tend to have low leverage in respect to change.

Over two years the Commission was able to encourage a more outward-looking approach. This led to schools making links beyond the local authority, with other schools and organisations that can support improvement efforts, including teaching schools, and through the MATS and faith-based partnerships.

As with our earlier projects, support for these developments was provided by a team of experienced advisers from outside the local authority with strong track records of success in challenging contexts. An emphasis on pace was achieved through each school's accelerated improvement board, which met monthly in a similar way to those in the Welsh schools.

Secondly, as in earlier projects, a strategic partnership board made up of headteachers and local authority staff was established to add value to what each partner is already doing to provide an effective education for every child and young person in the area. The board's work was guided by a vision of a high-performing system that is at the forefront of developments to find more effective ways of breaking the link between poverty, low attainment, and limited life chances.

Once again, a central feature was the idea of a self-improving local system: driven by school leaders and involving practitioners at all levels in taking collective responsibility for the quality of education across the authority. Importantly, the partnership board set out to involve all maintained schools, voluntary aided schools and academies, multi-academy trusts, and teaching schools, mobilising support from both within and outside the authority. In this way, it attempted to create a new type of partnership-based middle tier that could coordinate what became an increasingly complex map of networks and support possibilities. There was also an intention to continue commissioning challenge-type advisers to support schools experiencing difficulties.

These initiatives provided the basis of what could become a new, more powerful strategy for educational improvement in the local area. Together, they offered a more challenging strategy for supporting schools that makes better use of the expertise that is available, plus an overall mechanism for coordinating and monitoring the use of this strategy. However, as the period of the Commission came to an end, there was considerable uncertainty as to how such a strategy might be taken forward, not least because of the existence of a well-established collaborative culture which, perversely, tends to act as a barrier to change. This reminds us that whilst strengthened collaboration is essential to effective change, without other conditions it is insufficient as a strategy.

Conclusion

In this chapter I have argued that reforming education systems regarding inclusion and equity should be coordinated and supported locally. This means that national policy-makers must recognise that the details of policy implementation are not amenable to central regulation. Rather, these should be dealt with by those who are close to and, therefore, in a better position to understand local contexts.

Within the developments I have explored, the presence of experienced advisers who were able to provide local support for school-led improvement efforts proved to be crucial. In addition, they can broker and monitor forms of school-to-school support.

All of this leads to my sixth and final proposition, that *locally coordinated support and challenge based on the principles of inclusion and equity should be provided.*

Note

1 https://www.theguardian.com/education/2011/jan/25/school-improvement-city-challenge

8
THE CHALLENGE OF SUSTAINABILITY

In this concluding chapter, I draw together the six propositions developed in this book in order to suggest a framework that can be used to guide reforms for promoting inclusion and equity within educational systems. This framework is based on the idea that schools and their communities have untapped potential to improve their capacity for improving the participation, presence, and achievement of all of their students, particularly those who are vulnerable to marginalisation or exclusion. The challenge therefore is to mobilise this potential.

This reinforces my argument that educational improvement is a social process that involves practitioners in learning from one another, from their students, and from others involved in the lives of the young people they teach. Reform efforts need to create the conditions that will encourage such developments. However, these efforts are likely to meet contextual barriers. As I have explained, these relate to social, political, and cultural factors. My argument is that these difficulties can help move thinking forward, as argued by Thomas Edison, who famously said, *'I failed my way to success'.*

Using a recent system-wide reform development as an example, the chapter goes on to explain more about the nature of these difficulties. In so doing I address one of the greatest challenges facing attempts to bring about educational reform, that of achieving sustainable change. The chapter concludes with a discussion of the implications for the stances, roles, and methodologies of those in the research community.

Propositions

To recap, in this book, I have focused on the following agenda:

- How can education systems promote inclusion and equity?
- What are the barriers and how might they be overcome?
- What should be the roles of research and researchers?

The ideas that emerge from earlier chapters in relation to this agenda are as follows:

Proposition 1: Inclusion and Equity Should Be Seen as Principles That Inform All Educational Policies

These principles should focus in particular on those policies that are concerned with the curriculum, assessment processes, teacher education, accountability, and funding. Given the need to engage many stakeholders, clarity of purpose is crucial. With this in mind, strategies should be guided by the UNESCO mantra: *Every learner matters and matters equally*. In order to move policy and practice forward, it is also essential that evidence collected within an education system relates to the *'presence, participation and achievement'* of all students, with an emphasis placed on those groups of learners regarded to be 'at risk of marginalisation, exclusion or underachievement'. This rationale should also guide procedures for accountability.

Proposition 2: Barriers to the Presence, Participation, and Achievement of Learners Should Be Identified and Addressed

Progress in relation to inclusion and equity requires a move away from explanations of educational failure that focus on the characteristics of individual children and their families, towards an analysis of contextual barriers to participation and learning experienced by learners within schools. In this way, those students who do not respond to existing arrangements come to be regarded as 'hidden voices' who, under certain conditions, can encourage the improvement of schools. At the same time, evidence of various kinds is seen as a major driver to educational reforms.

The starting point for making decisions about the evidence to collect at the system level should be with agreed definitions of inclusion and equity. In other words, we must *measure what we value*, rather than is often the case, valuing what we can more easily measure.

Proposition 3: Schools Should Become Learning Communities where the Development of All Members Is Encouraged and Supported

Reforming education systems in relation to inclusion and equity requires coordinated and sustained efforts within schools, recognising that changing outcomes for vulnerable students are unlikely to be achieved unless there are changes in the attitudes, beliefs, and actions of adults. Therefore, the starting point must be with practitioners and policy-makers: enlarging their capacity to imagine what might be achieved and increasing their sense of accountability for bringing this about. This may also involve tackling negative assumptions, most often relating to expectations about certain groups of learners, their capabilities, and behaviours. Teacher professional development, stimulated by an engagement with evidence, is an essential factor in creating self-improving schools. The role of school leaders is to create the organisational conditions where all of this can happen.

Proposition 4: Partnerships Between Schools Should Be Developed in Order to Provide Mutual Challenge and Support

Research suggests that, under certain conditions, school-to-school collaboration can strengthen improvement processes by adding to the range of expertise made available. In particular, partnerships between schools have an enormous potential for fostering the capacity of education systems to respond to learner diversity. More specifically, they can help to reduce the polarisation of schools, to the particular benefit of those students who are marginalised at the edges of the system, and whose progress and attitudes are a cause for concern. All of this has implications for the various key stakeholders within education systems. In particular, teachers, especially those in senior positions, have to see themselves as having a wider responsibility for all children, not just those who attend their own schools. They also have to develop patterns of internal organisation that enable them to have the flexibility to cooperate with colleagues in other schools.

Proposition 5: Families and Other Community Partners Should Be Encouraged to Support the Work of Schools

The development of education systems that are effective for all children will only happen when what happens outside as well as inside a school changes. Indeed, there is encouraging evidence of what can happen when what schools do is aligned in a coherent strategy with the efforts of other community players – families, employers, community groups, universities, and public services. This does not necessarily mean schools doing more, but it does imply partnerships beyond the school, where partners multiply the impacts of each other's efforts. Place-based partnerships are a means of facilitating these forms of cooperation. School leaders have a crucial role in coordinating such arrangements, although other agencies can have important leadership roles.

Proposition 6: Locally Coordinated Support and Challenge Should Be Provided Based on the Principles of Inclusion and Equity

Developments regarding inclusion and equity should be led by schools that are self-improving. This means that policy-makers must recognise that the details of policy implementation are not amenable to central regulation. Rather, these should be dealt with by those who are close to and, therefore, in a better position to understand local contexts: teachers, principals, and community partners. This requires some form of local coordination. The presence of experienced advisers who can support and challenge school-led improvement is crucial. There is an important role for governments in creating the conditions for making such locally led improvements happen and providing the political mandate for ensuring their implementation. This also means that those who administer local education systems have to adjust their priorities and ways of working in response to improvement efforts that are led from within schools.

As I have stressed throughout this book, in making use of these six interconnected propositions it is vital to take account of contextual factors, some of which may create particular obstacles to their implementation. At the same time, we have to learn from things that don't work out in the way we had intended. As is sometimes argued, each of our mistakes has the potential to teach us something.

In relation to this argument, as an engaged researcher I have been much encouraged by the ideas of Peter Checkland (2012), who, after more than 40 years of active involvement in the field of system change, comments:

> ... it is disappointing to discover the rarity of detailed work to relate that thinking to 'particular, carefully sustained' work in actual situations and work leading to action 'traceable' back to the thinking. Only such work will, ultimately, demonstrate whether systems thinking is truly worth doing
>
> (p. 465)

With this in mind, in what follows I describe and reflect on my recent efforts with Chris Chapman and our colleagues at the University of Glasgow to apply the thinking presented in this book within a project to promote inclusion and equity across all the schools in the Scottish city of Dundee. Most importantly, this has created an opportunity to explore ways of achieving changes that are sustainable. For this purpose, I keep in mind a definition of sustainability provided by Askell-Williams and Koh (2020):

> .... the implementation of an effective initiative over a context-dependent timeframe leading to irreversible desirable system change.
>
> (p. 662)

The Dundee initiative has also provided a chance to refine my thinking regarding methodologies for using research to support such reform efforts, as I explain towards the end of the chapter.

A City-Wide Strategy

The Dundee strategy is informed by relevant international research literature, although this offers a somewhat depressing picture of the success of efforts to reform education systems, particularly when they are focused on the challenge of achieving equity. In essence, even those initiatives that showed promise tended to fade (see, e.g., Fullan, 2021; Payne, 2008; Sarason, 1990).

As a result of their review of literature on system change, Barrenechea, Beech and Rivas et al. (2023) conclude:

> ... attaining system-wide improvement is a complex endeavour that requires a variety of strategies and approaches that cannot be construed as a simple "silver-bullet" recipe.
>
> (p. 495)

This led the authors of the review to conclude:

> The need to invest in human capital, especially teachers, was the most salient specific driver in the literature we explored.
>
> (p. 490)

Bearing this argument in mind, the approach developed in Dundee is guided by a belief that system change must take account of contextual complexities. It involves a process of knowledge-generation, occurring when practitioner and researcher knowledge meet in particular sites, aimed at producing new knowledge about ways in which broad values might better be realised in future practice (Kerr and Ainscow, 2023). In practice, this means working across organisational, geographical, and professional boundaries, using inquiry and evidence to guide decision-making and progress towards a networked learning system (Madrid Miranda and Chapman, 2021).

Whilst this conceptualisation draws on notions of action research, and of research and development, it does not equate precisely with either approach. Unlike action research, it is not focused solely on achieving improvements in particular sites or specific 'projects', but seeks to generate transferable knowledge. Unlike research and development, it does not assume that the contribution of researchers to this process is prior to that of practitioners. In other words, researchers do not design practices that are then implemented by practitioners. Rather, we see our role as supporting practitioners in developing the best possible ways of promoting equity in a given situation. This also involves bringing to bear knowledge gained from prior research.

What emerges from this process is not a finely tuned set of practices that can be transferred wholesale to other sites. Rather, the practices developed in one site, together with their underpinning rationale, become an elaborated set of suggestions to be put forward for possible use in other contexts.

Every Dundee Learner Matters

Dundee is Scotland's fourth-largest city with a population of approximately 150,000 people. There are over 18,500 students in its schools and early years provision (nursery schools). Serving a context that has some areas of high-level economic disadvantage, the city has a history of challenges in terms of educational equity. The six propositions that emerged from the developments described in earlier chapters were important influences on what became known as Every Dundee Learner Matters (EDLM).

It is important to stress that the education system in Scotland operates in different ways to that of England. Responsibility for education there is fully devolved to the Scottish government and is administrated through 32 local authorities that have the legal responsibility for ensuring the quality of provision and school improvement. The overall situation in Scotland indicates positive features in regard to equity in that most students attend local schools that are part of the local authority. However, the performance of the education service has been a cause for concern over many years, particularly in relation to its impact on learners from economically disadvantaged backgrounds (Kintrea, 2021).

Scottish education policies are highly centralised, with local authorities acting as the delivery arms of nationally determined policies. This means that those in schools have limited space to make strategic decisions regarding actions that are needed to address local factors that are limiting the progress of some of their learners. As I will explain, this proved to be an important factor as the project in Dundee developed.

Evidence from our earlier programme of research had thrown light on the factors that seem to have limited educational progress in Scotland (Chapman and Ainscow, 2021). First of all, it suggests that national policies have tended to narrow the educational diet.

This involves a focus of attention on ways of improving a narrowly conceived range of outcomes, as signalled by the continual emphasis placed by Scottish Government on 'closing the poverty-related attainment gap'. As a result, there is a tendency to narrow the curriculum, focusing on literacy and numeracy, and allocate teaching time on those areas of learning that are seen as being most important. Significantly, this has occurred despite 'Curriculum for Excellence', an important reform to put in place a coherent 3-18 curriculum, first introduced in 2010.

At the same time, we have documented examples of how top-down patterns of decision-making act as barriers to change (Ainscow, Chapman and Hadfield, 2020).

All of this reflects what Humes (2020) refers to as a form of 'groupthink' that exists within the Scottish education system, leading to the recycling of approved forms of discourse.

The Strategy

EDLM is an ambitious attempt to overcome these contextual difficulties. In so doing, the aim is to bring about and learn from a change in the way a whole education system goes about addressing the challenge of addressing equity. The conditions for achieving this are encouraging in the sense that there is a high-level mandate for the strategy within Dundee and that members of our research team have well-established relationships with colleagues in the schools and local authority. On the other hand, the complexity of the strategy must be kept in mind, not least because it implies a collective effort to achieve common goals and because it was developed under the challenging circumstances imposed following the COVID pandemic.

Building on an earlier two-year pilot programme that involved 14 Dundee schools, EDLM was launched across the city in January 2021 following negotiations with senior officers in the local authority. As in earlier projects, the guiding vision is of a high-performing education system that is at the forefront of developments to find more effective ways of ensuring the education of all children and young people, particularly those who are most vulnerable to underachievement, marginalisation or exclusion. The strategy is driven by the principle of equity, defined as: *'A process of improving the presence, participation and progress of all children and young people in nurseries and schools by identifying and addressing contextual barriers'.*

It is envisioned that the development of a more inclusive and equitable system within the city will be achieved by building the capacity of schools to be self-improving. This involves developing a culture that embraces innovation and increasing practitioner leadership for working together using inquiry-based approaches to the development of practice, an approach that had proved to be effective in our earlier studies (e.g., Ainscow, Chapman and Hadfield, 2020; Ainscow et al., 2012a; Harris et al., 2017). This takes the form of a research-practice partnership:

> A long-term collaboration aimed at educational improvement or equitable transformation through engagement with research. These partnerships are intentionally organized to connect diverse forms of expertise and shift power relations in the research endeavour to ensure that all partners have a say in the joint work.
> (Farrell, Wentworth and Nayfack et al., 2021, p. 5)

Within the partnership, the overall methodology used is that of 'design-based implementation research'. Penuel and Riedy et al. (2020) explain that the broad aim of this approach is *'to support equitable change in educational systems such as states, districts, and learning ecosystems in communities through collaborative design and testing of solutions to persistent educational problems'* (p. 13). This approach is unusual in that all the partners involved have, to varying degrees, an involvement in both development and research. This is based on a belief that educational research findings will continue to be ignored, regardless of how well they are communicated, if they bypass the ways in which practitioners formulate the problems they face and the constraints within which they work (Ainscow et al., 2025).

What is distinctive here, too, is the focus on system-wide change. In practice, design-based approaches have usually operated more as technical exercises, limited to implementing small-scale curricular interventions (Cobb et al., 2003; Penuel et al., 2013; Tinoca et al., 2022).

Fishman et al. (2013) describe design-based implementation research as an approach that challenges educational researchers and practitioners to transcend traditional research/practice barriers in order to facilitate the design of educational interventions that are effective, sustainable, and scalable. They argue that the key principles of the approach are:

- A focus on persistent problems of practice from multiple stakeholders' perspectives;
- A commitment to iterative, collaborative design;
- A concern with developing theory and knowledge related to both classroom learning and implementation through systematic inquiry; and
- A concern with developing capacity for sustaining change in systems.

Design-based implementation research is one of a family of approaches that Yurkofsky et al. (2020) have labelled collectively as 'continuous improvement' methods They note that these share four characteristics:

- Grounding improvement efforts in local problems or needs;
- Empowering practitioners to take an active role in research and improvement;
- Engaging in iteration, which involves a cyclical process of action, assessment, reflection, and adjustment; and
- Striving to encourage change across schools and systems, not just individual classrooms.

Since the focus of the inquiry is usually defined by the engagement of the participants, careful consideration is required in determining who is included, and how and who will speak for whom, and who sets the research agenda. Therefore, negotiating power issues and the relationships between collaborating practitioners, stakeholders, and academics *'requires ethical probity where each party recognises, understands and respects mutual responsibilities'* (Campbell and Groundwater-Smith, 2007, p. 2).

The preoccupation with equity also means that the approach requires a particular concern to give voice to those who may be powerless or unheard in the decision-making processes, such as children and their families (Kerr and Ainscow, 2023). Moreover, actively engaging participants in inquiry *'problematises the question of who is researcher and who is researched, raising issues around anonymity, the 'ownership' of findings and dissemination'* (Locke, Alcorn and ONeill, 2013, p. 107).

Design Features

Drawing on evidence from our earlier studies and the insights of local practitioners, the EDLM strategy is built around a series of interconnected design features.

As in our earlier projects, a strategy group made up of headteachers coordinates and monitors the strategy. This group also has local authority and University representation.

Together, the design features shown in Figure 8.1 are intended to strengthen the capacity of schools to share ideas, knowledge, and practices

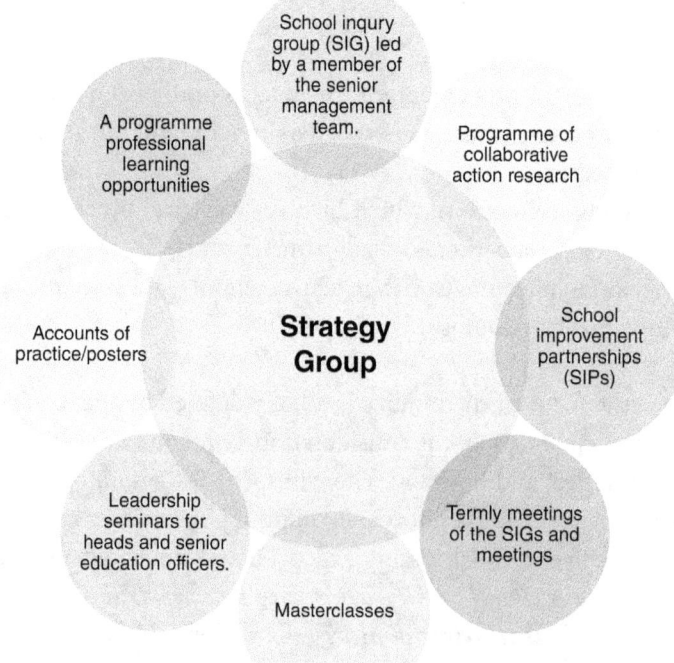

Figure 8.1 The EDLM design features

through collaboration amongst staff. This can also encourage new thinking and experimentation with alternative ways of working. Our earlier research shows that this can be stimulated through an engagement with the views of different stakeholders, bringing together the expertise of practitioners, the insights of students and families, and knowledge from academic research in ways that challenge taken-for-granted assumptions, not least in respect to the progress of vulnerable groups of learners (Ainscow et al., 2016).

In order to provide a clearly defined improvement agenda, EDLM is focussed on 'Three Ps':

- **Presence** – ensuring that all students attend regularly and promptly;
- **Participation** – creating a climate within schools where all students feel welcome and valued; and
- **Progress** – developing policies and practices that maximise the achievement and ambitions of all students.

This formulation echoes the experience of the earlier system change initiatives I have reported which suggested that easy-to-recall formulations can help busy colleagues to articulate to one other a sense of common purpose.

In developing the strategy in relation to these intended outcomes, the following assumptions were made:

- **Dundee schools already do well for many students** – the aim is to improve the learning of *all* children and young people; and
- **Within the schools and their communities there is considerable expertise that can be mobilised to address this agenda** – the aim therefore is to move this knowledge around so that it is made available to *all* students, in every school.

The strategy emphasises the following overall processes:

Contextual analysis. This involves determining barriers that are preventing the progress of some learners and the resources that can be mobilised in order to overcome these difficulties. It therefore requires an analysis of the best available evidence regarding the progress of young people across the city. This involves a particular emphasis on listening to the voices of students.

Collaborative action research. Emphasis is placed on stimulating innovation and creativity. This requires a new emphasis on evidence-based professional development carried out within schools.

Shared leadership. The strategy is led by schools for schools. This means that leadership is required at all levels of the system, not least at the classroom level.

Networking and collaboration. There are already many partnerships within Dundee that can be built upon. The strategy is focused on making sure that these are used effectively and that all schools are actively involved in ways that impact on classroom practices.

The involvement of the wider community. Building on successful experiences in Dundee during the COVID lockdown, this involves an emphasis on fostering improvements in health and wellbeing.

Our team of researchers from the University of Glasgow have supported these developments, whilst at the same time generating evidence to monitor their implementation and impact. This evidence is summarised in a series of evaluation reports[1].

Collaborative Action Research

The design features include an approach to school-based collaborative action research that is explained in a guide that all the schools have followed, albeit to varying degrees. Adopting what we see as a tight/loose stance, this involves attempts to make better use of the existing expertise of teachers and other stakeholders. Importantly, it requires schools to have greater flexibility, within a common framework, to determine how resources are used to address local circumstances. It also builds on research which suggests that when teachers are involved in decision-making this is likely to promote a stronger culture for learning within educational settings (Schleicher, 2010).

A significant feature of the approach presented in the EDLM guide is the emphasis it places on taking strategic decisions to focus attention on those learners thought to be 'missing out' within existing arrangements (Ainscow, 2024a). In adopting this perspective, there was a concern that this might lead to narrowly focused efforts to 'fix' students seen as being in some sense inadequate. With this in mind, the intention was that collecting and engaging with evidence about these learners and their experiences would lead to a re-focusing of attention around contextual factors that are acting as barriers to their participation and learning, as occurred in earlier studies (e.g., Ainscow et al., 2012a). In this way, it was hoped that 'double-loop learning' would occur, such that the projects carried out will gradually become school improvement efforts that have the potential to benefit many if not all students.

To explain, Argyris and Schon (1996) argue that organisations, such as schools, are capable of learning, but to different extents and, indeed, at different levels. What they refer to as 'single-loop learning' takes the form of what in an educational context might be called the improvement of existing practices but without any fundamental reconsideration of the assumptions upon which those practices are based. On the other hand, 'double-loop learning' asks questions about the underlying aims of practice and about the implicit theories which underpin it. Accounts of practice provided in the EDLM guide illustrate a range of examples of what this might look like but, subsequently, each school has developed its own approach, taking account of local challenges.

The introduction of the strategy for school development outlined in the EDLM guide has significant implications for the roles of local authority staff in ways that draw on the experiences of the challenge advisers discussed in Chapter Seven. In particular, it has required them to adjust their ways of working in response to the development of improvement strategies that are led from within schools. Specifically, their task is to monitor, support, and challenge schools in relation to the agreed goals of collaborative activities, whilst senior staff within schools share responsibility for the overall management of improvement efforts. Another of their roles involves collaboration with university staff in acting as 'critical friends', questioning colleagues in the schools in ways that will help facilitate such rethinking processes. In this way, the EDLM strategy aims to enhance the facilitation role of local authority staff in building leadership capacity and effective collaboration within and across schools.

In taking on such roles, local authority staff are positioned as guardians of improved outcomes for all young people and their families – protectors of a more collegiate approach but not as managers of day-to-day activities. As mentioned in Chapter 7, this means that *the job of schools is to improve themselves and the role of the local authority is to make sure that this happens*. In moving forward, it was important to document the progress of this radical change in thinking and its impact on practices in schools.

Engaging with Evidence

In planning a way forward, we found it helpful to draw on the ideas of Michael Fullan (2007). He suggests that improvement strategies should be planned in relation to three overlapping phases: *initiation*, which involves scrutinising evidence in order to determine priorities for action; *implementation*, involving supported action in relation to agreed goals; and *institutionalisation*, in order to ensure that changes become part of the culture of an organisation and, therefore, maintained.

As I have explained, the initiation phase of the Dundee initiative took place during a time of unprecedented challenges, as the schools struggled to cope with the continuing impact of the COVID pandemic. During the period that followed, our research group from the University of Glasgow collected and analysed evidence regarding the implementation of the strategy using the following methods:

- Observations within schools, and during meetings and events;
- Group interviews;
- Social network analysis surveys; and
- A scrutiny of statistical evidence and practitioner-generated evidence.

These data indicated high levels of implementation of the strategy across the city's schools. Despite the unfavourable context, the following arrangements were successfully introduced:

- Across the Dundee education system there is widespread awareness of the strategy and what it has set out to achieve;
- All schools have established one or more school inquiry groups (SIGs);
- These groups have used collaborative action research to identify and address barriers to the presence, participation, and progress of some of their students;
- All schools are members of a school improvement partnership (SIP) set up to share experiences and encourage innovations;
- Education officers and members of the research team have worked together to support these school-led improvement efforts; and
- A programme of workshops and conferences has taken place to provide support and advice for key people in the field.

At the same time, the evidence we generated has shown tensions that are always a possibility when introducing such a massive change. For example, there were examples of how proposals for development can, at times, be endangered by what Reynolds (1991) refers to as 'cling-ons' to past practices. There was also evidence of schools looking to find solutions to the challenges they face externally, rather than through drawing on the expertise that exists within their school communities through collaborative action research.

The evidence also threw light on the challenges of getting system-wide commitment. Talking about this, a secondary headteacher commented: *'It can't be every Dundee learner matters in certain schools only'*.

The second and third years of EDLM were seen as the implementation phase. This meant moving the strategy on from what might seem like a 'project', running alongside the core business of schools, to an approach that is at the centre of each school's improvement agenda. With this in mind, the following actions were taken:

- Attention was given to ensuring that school leaders are taking a central role in using inquiry-based strategies to strengthen classroom practices;

- Peer inquiry procedures were introduced that involve senior staff in schools visiting each other to support and challenge their efforts;
- A professional development programme was introduced to support local authority officers in developing their roles in response to improvement strategies that are increasingly led by schools themselves; and
- Occasional research summaries were used to inform all stakeholders regarding progress in implementing the strategy.

At the same time, further efforts were made to develop the capacity of the headteachers within the strategy group to take on the role of system leaders. During the third year, this led to a recognition that school attendance had become an increasing concern across the city. With this in mind, the strategy group took action to encourage schools to collaborate in finding ways of addressing this challenge.

Developing Inclusive Cultures

The evidence we have generated indicates that the EDLM strategy has brought about significant changes in thinking and practice in schools across Dundee. There is also evidence of impact on student outcomes, as indicated by statistical evidence generated by the local authority in the summer of 2024. This included: improvements in overall school attendance; and higher gains in literacy and numeracy at the primary school stage than across the rest of Scotland. Understandably, measurable impacts on student outcomes in the secondary sector are taking longer to achieve.

The big challenge now is to ensure that these improvements become sustainable and have an even greater impact on student outcomes. This implies developments in organisational cultures based on forms of collaboration that encourage and support problem-solving.

Traditional school cultures, supported by rigid organisational arrangements, teacher isolation, and high levels of specialisms amongst staff who are geared to predetermined tasks, are often in trouble when faced with unexpected circumstances (Hargreaves, 1995). On the other hand, the presence of learners who are not suited to the existing 'menu' of a school provides some encouragement to explore a more collegiate culture within which practitioners are supported in experimenting with new teaching responses. In this way, problem-solving activities may gradually become the reality-defining functions that are the culture of a school that is committed to finding ways of reaching out to all of its students.

Based on the evidence we collected, particularly the information that emerged from practitioners' collaborative action research activities, in and across schools, we have encouraged schools to map their progress in relation to an overall theoretical framework, adapted from an earlier study focusing on school culture (Ainscow, Hargreaves and Hopkins, 1995):

The framework (see figure 8.2) is designed in relation to two overall factors:

- **Innovation** – This concept tends to be rather inexplicitly defined in the educational change literature. Thinking about charter school innovations in the United States, Preston et al. (2012) put it this way:

    'In defining innovation, we submit that educational practices cannot be deemed innovative in an absolute sense, but innovations must be considered in terms of their relative prevalence in a local and state context'.
- **Inquiring stance** – This implies a more active, questioning approach to development in relation to evidence collected within a school.

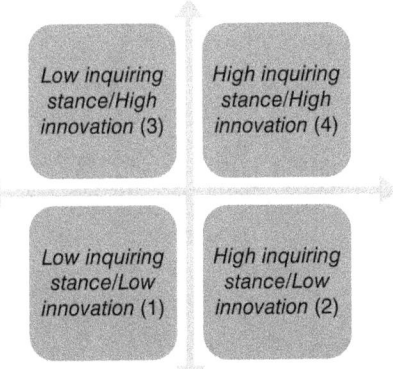

Figure 8.2 A theoretical framework

In exploring this framework, exemplars can be developed for each of the quadrants:

1 *Low inquiring stance/Low innovation* – A school that is relatively stable but has limited capacity to use evidence to stimulate change
2 *High Inquiring stance/Low innovation* – A school that is engaging with evidence but has low capacity to make change
3 *Low inquiring stance/High innovation* – A school that is developing but has a low capacity for using evidence to encourage change
4 *High inquiring stance/High innovation* – A school that is motivated to improve and knows how to use evidence to stimulate change

This framework has been used by school leaders to think about where they are in relation to the process of change and what steps are needed to move forward. In this way, the aim is for them to become the co-designers and, simultaneously, bearers of a new culture of inquiry-based collaboration within their school's communities of practice.

More Barriers

An important feature of the Dundee initiative is the emphasis it places on bottom-up leadership within a context of a top-down political mandate. As I have explained, evidence from both formal research and school-based inquiry has been used to inform these developments to a considerable degree. However, we have found that injecting ideas from research into such developments has sometimes been difficult because of a series of interconnected barriers.

Some of the barriers relate to political factors, something that can be anticipated within such a centralised national policy context. For example, despite EDLM being recognised as the local authority's improvement strategy, schools still get occasional mixed messages about what should be their priorities. In particular, ideas from national strategies continue to create some degree of confusion. One headteacher explained: *'We have four projects running but only one of them is focused on EDLM. The other three projects are running alongside each other and it's just a case that we're focused on this one in terms of paperwork and making sure that everything's sort of evaluated fully'.*

There are also cultural factors, created by local traditions and the expectations of those involved as to what is possible. For example, the extent to which schools have focused on those learners who are currently 'missing out' has continued to vary within a context where overall attainment targets continue to dominate their priorities. Meanwhile, discussions still focus on the continuing impact of patterns that developed during the COVID period, not least about school attendance. For example, a secondary deputy headteacher commented: *'Young people have sussed it out – they don't have to be in school all the time, you know. And, actually, I would say, well do they, do they really need to be in school all the time?'* Teacher turnover has also created barriers, as noted by a nursery school headteacher: *I've not had a static staff team in four years.*

Other barriers relate to the traditional ways in which decisions are made. So, for example, at a meeting of the strategy group to plan a forthcoming event for headteachers, one head commented: *'I hope we don't have the graveyard spot again'*. His point was that, traditionally, these meetings usually consisted of a series of rather formal presentations made by senior local authority officers or, occasionally, by government representatives, during which the participants rarely spoke. The sense of the hand of central government behind some of this was evident at a meeting of heads to explain the need for so-called 'stretch aims', when a senior local authority officer explained, *'This is what we have been told to say'*.

All of this creates a context within which school leaders perceive themselves as waiting for a lead from 'above'. For example, commenting on the situation in secondary schools led one head teacher to explain, *'They are waiting for someone to tell them what to do'*.

In relation to this concern, a meeting held in November 2023, now re-titled as 'headteacher learning days', was an important turning point in the implementation of EDLM. In particular, it signalled a shift in tone and emphasis from previous sessions that had tended to focus on the transmission of information and messages from national/local government. Led by members of the strategy group, the day used examples of practices from schools to encourage participants to reflect on developments in their own organisations as a stimulus for round table discussions. Commenting on the concern with school attendance that had emerged, a senior local authority officer noted: *'The answers are in this room'*.

These relatively minor events can be seen as 'critical incidents', defined as unplanned and unanticipated moments that provoke reflection. As such, they draw attention to taken-for-granted assumptions that inform actions within a particular context. In particular, they remind us of how historical factors, leading to taken-for-granted assumptions and existing ways of working, can act as hidden barriers to the introduction of new ideas. The challenge for engaged researchers is to find ways of making sense of the cultural complexities involved in order that sustainable change can be achieved. This points us towards the importance of cultural factors.

Organisational Cultures

As I explained in Chapter 4, cultures are about the deeper levels of basic assumptions and beliefs that are shared by members of an organisation, operating unconsciously to define how they view themselves and their working contexts. There is, therefore, an inevitable historical dimension that is always there when, as outsiders, we become involved in a new context. The problem is that these factors may not be articulated, since they are largely taken for granted amongst those involved. Making sense of them from an outsider's perspective is, therefore, a major challenge.

A helpful commentary on this in relation to Scotland is provided by Walter Humes (2020), who draws on what Bantock calls *'the parochialism of the present'*, a condition that focuses on current preoccupations alone and fails to consider what might be learned from past experiences. For example, referring to major curriculum changes that have been introduced in Scotland over recent years, Humes argues that if those responsible for directing the reform had paid more attention to the lessons of history, things might have been different. Previous reforms, he suggests, although modest in scale, had all encountered difficulties and had taken longer to implement than had been hoped. Moreover, these reforms had been centrally directed, with limited scope for teacher involvement. Quoting the curriculum expert

Lawrence Stenhouse, Humes explains that there can be no successful curriculum development without teacher development.

Humes goes on to explain how historical factors can influence reactions of stakeholders, such as teachers, school leaders, and local administrators, to proposals for change of the sort we have introduced in Dundee. In so doing, he suggests that expressing views which may not accord with official policy can carry significant risks. In some schools and local authorities, he argues, this may lead to a climate of fear. And, of course, such feelings may be well below the surface, influencing what happens in subtle ways, as in the case of the head teacher who raised the issue of the 'graveyard spot'.

The implication is that the barriers experienced in implementing the EDLM strategy may be a result of bumping up against such taken-for-granted assumptions. It occurs to me, too, that this may be a particular strong feature in this relatively small education system, where there are close social links amongst players. I am also conscious that there are significant numbers of these colleagues who have lived and worked in Dundee for a long time. Meanwhile, Kintrea (2021) argues: *'Beneath the calm surface of Scotland's consensual and seemingly inclusive approach lie significant inequalities' (p. x)*.

The Roles of Research and Researchers

The idea that educational research can simply be 'applied to practice' and have direct effects in the field has now largely been abandoned, even though it may still be held by some researchers, who, it has been suggested, *'seem surprised or even dismayed that their work is not immediately adopted into policy or practice'* (Levin, 2011, p. 17). Meanwhile, there have been numerous efforts to bring research, policy, and practice closer together. In so doing, this has often involved 'research and development', a tradition across a wide range of disciplines in which research sets out to solve problems generated by practice. The assumption, then, is that practitioners will implement the findings and that implementation will itself be researched, so that solutions might be refined. The implication being that educational research does speak to issues of practice, if only the right people will listen.

As I have explained, the initiative in Dundee adopts a different perspective. This involves:

- Efforts to develop thinking and practice in relation to the principle of equity;
- Practitioners inquiring into their own practices, on an assumption that such processes would impact on the values on which they act; and
- University researchers acting as supporters and critical friends of practitioners and local policy-makers.

Over time, we came to understand that the process of acting on these elements as one in which researcher and practitioner knowledge meet in particular contexts to produce new understandings of ways in which broad values of equity might be better realised in practice.

All of this has particularly important implications for those of us in the research community. With this in mind, I seek to contribute to ongoing debates about finding ways of ensuring that educational research has an impact on thinking and practice in the field.

Developing a Methodology

At this stage, it is important to say something more about the evolution of the stance I adopt. In 2004, Alan Dyson and I founded the Centre for Equity in Education at the University of Manchester. The Centre was established with a remit to work in high-poverty places, in the United Kingdom and internationally, with schools, communities, and policy-makers, in response to the challenges and opportunities arising in particular complex localised contexts (Ainscow et al., 2009). The overall direction of the Centre's programme of work was monitored and guided by a 'thinktank' that met termly. This was made up of well-connected players in the education field, including a local authority officer, headteachers, representatives of other disciples within the University, a retired school inspector and, occasionally, various eminent academics from other universities. Regular reports were published, including manifestos prior to elections that were designed to have an impact on community debates.

What made the Centre's approach particularly distinctive, however, was its explicit intention to blend together research and development. It set out to do this not through some top-down, linear pathways, where those working and living in particular places would be expected to implement recommendations arising from university-led research. Rather, it involved us in working alongside those leading local efforts to develop more equitable arrangements.

As I explained in Chapter Six, a distinctive methodological approach evolved through the Centre's work, which we have recently termed 'design-based equity research' (Kerr and Ainscow, 2023). Within this approach, the central tenet of *'working with, rather than working on',* derived from our much earlier work within the IQEA project, is retained (Ainscow and Southworth, 1996). This requires a sustained working relationship between researchers and practitioners, founded on a shared purpose and values stance. In these contexts, practitioners own and lead developments, and researchers, as 'critical friends', elucidate and support ongoing development processes, bringing to this their knowledge and expertise. As expressed in one of our Centre's working maxims, our aim is to work in ways that allow us to be 'at the table' when policy decisions are debated, even if others at the table do not always like what we have to say.

We have found that this way of working can sometimes have an uncomfortable relationship with the wider community of academic peers. For example, we have struggled at times even to have our work recognised as 'research', finding ourselves categorised either as consultants, as doing 'development work', seen as a non-research activity, or, more simply, in the words of one colleague, *'messing around in schools'.*

Within the approach I have explained, academic researchers count as secondary actors; i.e., they can act on that situation but only through the mediation of practitioners, who are the primary actors. However, researchers can make two distinctive contributions. First of all, by providing access to resources (e.g., research skills, relevant literature, experience in other contexts) that practitioners might, in principle, have access to, but which, in practice, are often denied them. And secondly, researchers are defined by their distance from practice and therefore from the assumptions on which practice is based.

In other words, we belong to a socio-cultural group that is not that of practitioners, and which is therefore able to draw on different sets of assumptions and open up further possibilities for action.

The different roles and socio-cultural contexts of practitioners and academics create a complex set of power relations that have to be factored into the process explicitly. Practitioners derive their power from being primary actors: they can cause things to happen, or to cease to happen, in a way that is denied to academics. Meanwhile, academic researchers derive their power from standing at a distance: they can problematise the actions of practitioners (Chapman and Ainscow, 2019).

At their most productive, these power relationships lead to dialogue in which the academics' views are informed by the realities of practice, and practitioners' views change in response to 'outsider' critique. At the least productive, academics mistake their distant position for superiority and claim moral and intellectual authority over practitioners, while practitioners dismiss academics as ignorant and resist their critiques. Managing these relationships is crucial to any successful process of collaboration between practitioners and researchers.

Research-practice Partnerships

Reflecting further on these ideas, I connect my work to the growing movement towards building research-practice partnerships, both in the United Kingdom (see, e.g., Sharples, Maxwell and Coldwell, 2023) and internationally (see Sjölund et al., 2022). This momentum has largely been fuelled by the recognition that educational change and the construction of more equitable education structures require different educational actors to be active participants in the process, in order to create new forms of knowledge and feed these into systems through social learning approaches (Ishimaru, 2020; Spillane et al., 2019).

For university researchers, the prolonged contact that such partnerships involve enables them to gain a detailed knowledge of the locality, as well as the institutions and systems – and the assumptions inherent within these – that structure local activity. This time spent in the field allows the researcher to identify and explore problems of practice, as well as test out and refine potential solutions, in ways that create knowledge and understanding as to *'why, how, and under what conditions programmes and policies work'* (Gutiérrez and Penuel, 2014, p. 1).

Meanwhile, for practitioners, this prolonged contact not only enables them to understand better aspects of their local context by confronting their own professional assumptions, but they are also likely to have a greater understanding of research findings generated where they have been actively involved in this process. Furthermore, they have ready access to guidance and support in terms of applying these research-informed solutions into their local development strategies.

In this regard, such partnerships are well-positioned to develop research that directly relates to local issues and to do so in ways that take account of particular contexts, as well as local educational experiences and outcomes. Underpinning all this, for all the groups involved, the prolonged contact of working alongside each other enables all those taking part in the partnership to develop strong, long-lasting relationships, mutuality and trust, founded on shared values, and a shared commitment to key outcomes (Penuel, Coburn and Gallagher, 2013).

Within such contexts, I see my role as providing support to practitioners in developing the best possible ways of promoting inclusion and equity within a given situation. Moreover, what emerges from practitioners' attempts to act on these ideas is not a finely tuned and context-independent set of practices which can be transferred wholesale to other sites. Rather, the practices developed in one site, together with their underpinning rationale, become an elaborated set of propositions to be put forward for consideration in other contexts.

I should add that, during this era, university researchers are experiencing their own barriers in trying to contribute directly to changes in thinking within the field of education. This is summed up by Checkland and Poulter (2020):

> As governments around the world seek to turn universities into imitation bureaucratic corporations, while measuring research output in terms of publications, the pressure to publish is immense; so academics take the easy option: writing papers about other papers, rather than describing engagements with complex reality.
>
> (p. 469)

Final Thoughts

The experiences summarised in this book point to the sorts of conditions that are needed in order to use processes of collaboration between policy-makers, practitioners, and researchers to reform education systems in relation to inclusion and equity. As I have explained, the approach is based on the idea that schools and their communities have untapped potential to improve their capacity for improving the achievement of all of their students, particularly those who are vulnerable to marginalisation or exclusion. The challenge is to mobilise this potential.

This reinforces my argument that educational change is a social process that involves practitioners in learning from one another, from their students, and from others involved in the lives of the young people they teach. And, as I have explained, an engagement with evidence can be a powerful catalyst for making this happen. Reform efforts have to build on this thinking.

Note

1 For example: https://nsee.org.uk/research-that-makes-a-difference-lessons-from-dundee/

References

Adonis, A. (2012) *Education, education, education, reforming England's schools*. London: Biteback Publishing.
Ainscow, M. (1999) *Understanding the development of inclusive schools*. London: Routledge.
Ainscow, M., Booth, T. and Dyson, A. (2004) 'Understanding and developing inclusive practices in schools: a collaborative action research network', International Journal of Inclusive Education, 8(2), 125–140.
Ainscow, M. (2005) 'Developing inclusive education systems: what are the levers for change?', *Journal of Educational Change*, 6, pp. 109–124.
Ainscow, M. (2007) 'Taking an inclusive turn', *Journal of Research in Special Educational Needs*, 7(1), pp. 3–7.
Ainscow, M. (2010) 'Achieving excellence and equity: reflections on the development of practices in one local district over 10 years', *School Effectiveness and School Improvement*, 21(1), pp. 75–91.
Ainscow, M. (2012) 'Moving knowledge around: strategies for fostering equity within educational systems', *Journal of Educational Change*, 13(3), pp. 289–310.
Ainscow, M. (2013) 'Developing more equitable education systems: reflections on a three-year improvement initiative', in Farnsworth, V. and Solomon, Y. (eds.) *What works in education? Bridging theory and practice in research*. London: Routledge.
Ainscow, M. (2015) *Towards self-improving school systems: lessons from a city challenge*. London: Routledge.
Ainscow, M. (2016a) *Struggles for equity in education: the selected works of Mel Ainscow*. London: Routledge World Library of Educationalists series.
Ainscow, M. (2016b) 'Collaboration as a strategy for promoting equity in education: possibilities and barriers', *Journal of Professional Capital and Community*, 1(2), pp. 159–172.

REFERENCES

Ainscow, M. (2020) 'Promoting inclusion and equity in education: lessons from international experiences', *The Nordic Journal of Studies on Educational Policy*, 6(1), pp. 7–16.

Ainscow, M. (2023) 'Promoting equity within education systems. Lessons from Great Britain', *Forum*, 65(1), pp. 87–97.

Ainscow, M. (2024a) *Developing inclusive schools: pathways to success*. Routledge.

Ainscow, M. (2024b) *Every learner matters and matters equally: making education inclusive. Paper commissioned by UNESCO for the celebration of the 30th Anniversary of the Salamanca Statement*. Paris: UNESCO.

Ainscow, M., Armstrong, P., Hughes, B.C. and Rayner, S.M. (2023) *Turning the Tide: a study of place-based partnerships*. The Staff College (https://thestaffcollege.uk/publications/turning-the-tide/)

Ainscow, M., Booth, T. and Dyson, A. (2006) 'Inclusion and the standards agenda: negotiating policy pressures in England', *International Journal of Inclusive Education*, 10(4–5), pp. 295–308.

Ainscow, M., Booth, T., Dyson, A., with Farrell, P., Frankham, J., Gallannaugh, F., Howes, A. and Smith, R. (2006) *Improving schools, developing inclusion*. London: Routledge.

Ainscow, M., Calderón-Almendros, I., Duk, C. and Viola, M. (2014) Using professional development to promote inclusive education in Latin America: possibilities and challenges. *Professional Development in Education*, 1–18. https://doi.org/10.1080/19415257.2024.2427285

Ainscow, M., Chapman, C. and Hadfield, M. (2020) *Changing education systems: a research-based approach*. Routledge.

Ainscow, M., Crow, M., Dyson, A., Goldrick, S., Kerr, K., Lennie, C., Miles, S., Muijs, D. and Skyrme, J. (2007) *Equity in education: new directions: the second annual report of the centre for equity in education, University of Manchester*. Manchester: Centre for Equity in Education.

Ainscow, M., Dyson, A., Goldrick, S. and Kerr, K. (2009) 'Using research to foster equity and inclusion within the context of new labour educational reforms', in Chapman, G.M. and Gunter, H. (eds.) *Radical reforms: perspectives on an era of educational change*. London: Routledge.

Ainscow, M., Dyson, A., Goldrick, S. and West, M. (2012a) *Developing equitable education systems*. London: Routledge.

Ainscow, M., Dyson, A., Goldrick, S. and West, M. (2012b) 'Making schools effective for all: rethinking the task', *School Leadership & Management*, 32(3), pp. 197–213.

Ainscow, M., Dyson, A. and Hopwood, L. and with Thomson, S. (2016) *Primary schools responding to diversity: barriers and possibilities*. New York: Cambridge Primary Review Trust.

Ainscow, M., Forbes, C. and Madrid Miranda, R. (2025) Using research to promote equity within education systems: roles, challenges and possibilities, in *BERA-Sage handbook on research-informed education practice and policy*. London: Sage.

REFERENCES

Ainscow, M., Hargreaves, D.H. and Hopkins, D. (1995) 'Mapping the process of change in schools: the development of six new research techniques', *Evaluation and Research in Education*, 9(2), pp. 75–89.

Ainscow, M. and Hopkins, D. (1992) 'Aboard the 'Moving School', *Educational Leadership*, 50(3), pp. 79–81.

Ainscow, M. and Howes, A. (2007) 'Working together to improve urban secondary schools: a study of practice in one city', *School Leadership and Management*, 27(3), pp. 285–300.

Ainscow, M., Howes, A. and Tweddle, D.A. (2006) 'Moving practice forward at the districtlevel', in Ainscow, M. and West, M. (eds.) *Improvement in urban schools: leadership and collaboration*. Maidenhead: Open University Press.

Ainscow, M. and Kaplan, I. (2005) 'Using evidence to encourage inclusive school development: possibilities and challenges', *Australasian Journal of Special Education*, 29(2), pp. 12–21.

Ainscow, M. and Messiou, K. (2017) 'Engaging with the views of students to promote inclusion in education', *Journal of Educational Change*, 19(1), pp. 1–17.

Ainscow, M., Muijs, D. and West, M. (2006) 'Collaboration as a strategy for improving schools in challenging circumstances', *Improving Schools*, 9(3), pp. 192–202.

Ainscow, M. and Muncey, J. (1989) *Meeting individual needs in the primary school*. London: Fulton.

Ainscow, M., Nicolaidou, M., and West, M. (2003) Supporting schools in difficulties: The role of school-to-school cooperation. NFER Topic 30, 1–4.

Ainscow, M. and Southworth, G. (1996) 'School improvement: a study of the roles of leaders and external consultants', *School Effectiveness and School Improvement*, 7(3), pp. 229–251.

Ainscow, M. and Tweddle, D.A. (1979) *Preventing classroom failure*. London: Fulton.

Ainscow, M. and Tweddle, D.A. (1984) *Early learning skills analysis*. London: Fulton.

Ainscow, M. and Viola, M. (2023) 'Developing inclusive and equitable education systems: some lessons from Uruguay', *International Journal of Inclusive Education*. https://doi.org/10.1080/13603116.2023.2279556

Ainscow, M. and West, M.(eds.) (2006) *Improving urban schools: leadership and collaboration*. Open University Press.

Alves, I., Campos Pinto, P. and Pinto, T.J. (2020) Developing inclusive education in Portugal: evidence and challenges. *Prospects* https://doi.org/10.1007

Anderson, T. and Shattuck, J. (2012) 'Design-based research - a decade of progress in education research', *Educational Researcher*, 41(1), pp. 16–25.

Anyon, J. (2005) What "counts" as educational policy? Notes toward a new paradigm. *Harvard Educational Review*, 75, pp. 65–88.

REFERENCES

Argyris, C. and Schon, D. (1996) *Organisational learning II: theory, method and practice*. Reading MA: Addison Wesley.

Armstrong, P. and Ainscow, M. (2018) 'School-to-school support within a competitive education system: views from the inside', *School Effectiveness, School Improvement*, 29(4), pp. 614–633.

Askell-Williams, H. and Koh, G.A. (2020) 'Enhancing the sustainability of school improvement initiatives', *School Effectiveness and School Improvement*, 31(4), pp. 660–678.

Au, W. (2009) *Unequal by design: high-stakes testing and the standardization of inequality*. London: Routledge.

AuCoin, A., Porter, G.L. and Baker-Korotkov, K., 2020. New Brunswick's journey to inclusive education. *Prospects*. https://doi.org/10.1007/s11125-020-09508-8.

Avalos, B. (2011) 'Teacher professional development in teaching and teacher education over ten years', *Teaching and Teacher Education*, 27, pp. 10–20.

Barrenechea, I., Beech, J. and Rivas, A. (2023) 'How can education systems improve? A systematic literature review', *Journal of Educational Change*, 24, pp. 479–499.

Biesta, G.J.J. (2010) 'Why 'What Works' still won't work: from evidence-based education to value-based education', *Studies in Philosophy of Education*, 29, pp. 491–503.

Black-Hawkins, K. and Florian, L. (2012) 'Classroom teachers craft knowledge of their inclusive practice', *Teachers and Teaching: Theory and Practice*, 18(5), pp. 567–584.

Bleicher, R.E. (2014) 'A collaborative action research approach to professional learning', *Professional Development in Education*, 40(5), p. 802e821.

Booth, T. and Ainscow, M.(eds.) (1998) *From them to us: an international study of inclusion in education*. London: Routledge.

Booth, T. and Ainscow, M. (2000) *The index for inclusion*. Bristol: Centre for Studies on Inclusive Education.

Bubb, S., Crossley-Holland, J., Cordiner, J., Cousin, S. and Earley, P. (2019) *Understanding the middle tier: comparative costs of academy and LA-maintained school systems*. London: Sara Bubb Associates.

Burgess, S. (2014) *Understanding the success of London's schools*. Bristol: CMPO Working Paper No.14/333.

Butler, D.L. and Schnellert, L. (2012) 'Collaborative inquiry in teacher professional development', *Teaching and Teacher Education*, 28, 1206e1220

Cain, T. and Milovic, S. (2010) 'Action research as a tool of professional development of advisers and teachers in Croatia', *European Journal of Teacher Education*, 33(1), p. 19e30.

Calderón-Almendros, I., Ainscow, M., Bersanelli, S. and Molina-Toledo, P. (2020) 'Educational inclusion and equity in Latin America: an analysis of the challenges', *Prospects*, 49, pp. 169–186.

Campbell, S. and Groundwater-Smith(eds.) (2007) *An ethical approach to practitioner research: dealing with issues and dilemmas in action research*. London: Routledge.

Carr, C., Brown, S. and Morris, M. (2017) *Assessing the contribution of schools challenge Cymru to outcomes achieved by pathways to success schools*. Cardiff: Welsh Government.

Chapman, C. and Ainscow, M. (2019) 'Using research to promote equity within education systems: possibilities and barriers', *British Education Research Journal*, 45(3), pp. 899–917.

Chapman, C. and Ainscow, M. (eds.) (2021) *Educational equity: Pathways to success*. London: Routledge.

Checkland, P. (2012) 'Four conditions for serious systems thinking and action', *Systems Research and Behavioral Science*, 29, pp. 465–469.

Checkland, P. and Poulter, J. (2020) 'Soft systems methodology', in Reynolds, M. and Holwell, S. (eds.) *Systems approaches to making change: a practical guide*. London: Springer.

Claeys, A., Kempton, J. and Paterson, C. (2014) *Regional challenges: a collaborative approach to improving education*. London: Centre Forum.

Clarke, P., Ainscow, M. and West, M. (2006) 'Learning from difference: some reflections on school improvement projects in three countries', in Harris, A. and Crispeels, J.H. (eds.) *Improving schools and education systems*. London: Routledge, pp. 77–89.

Cobb, P., Confrey, J., DiSessa, A., Lehrer, R. and Schauble, L. (2003) Design experiments in educational research. *Educational Researcher*, 32(1), pp. 9–13.

Committee of Public Accounts (2022) Academies Sector Annual Report and Accounts 2019/20 – Report Summary. London: UK Parliament.

Cordingley, P., Bell, M., Evans, D. and Firth, A. (2005) The impact of collaborative CPD on classroom teaching and learning, in Research evidence in education library. London: EPPI-Centre, Social Science Research Unit, Institute of Education, University of London.

Dobbie, W. and Fryer, R.G. (2009) *Are high-quality schools enough to close the achievement gap? Evidence from a bold social experiment in Harlem*. Cambridge: Harvard University.

Drever, A., McLean, J., and Lowden, K. (2021) 'Focusing on place: Working beyond the school gate', in Chapman, C. and Ainscow, M. (eds.) *Educational equity: Pathways to success*. London: Routledge.

Duk, C., Blanco, R., Zecchetto, F., Capell, C.Y. and López, M. (2021) 'Desarrollo profesional docente para la inclusión: Investigación acción colaborativa a través de estudios de clase en escuelas Chilenas', *Revista Latinoamericana de Educación Inclusiva*, 15(2), pp. 67–95.

Dyson, A., Gallannaugh, F. and Millward, A. (2003) 'Making space in the standards agenda: developing inclusive practices in schools', *European Educational Research Journal*, 2(2), pp. 228–244.

Dyson, A., Howes, A. and Roberts, B. (2004) 'What do we really know about inclusive schools? A systematic review of the research evidence', in Mitchell, D. (ed.) *Special educational needs and inclusive education: major themes in education*. London: Routledge.

Dyson, A. and Kerr, K. (2013) *Developing children's zones for England: What's the evidence?* London: Save the Children.

Elliott Major, L. and Briant, E. (2023) *Equity in education: levelling the playing field of learning – a practical guide for teachers.* London: John Catt.

Elmore, R.F. (2004) *School reform from the inside out: policy, practice, and performance.* Harvard Education Press.

Elmore, R.F., Peterson, P.L. and McCarthy, S.J. (1996) *Restructuring in the classroom: teaching, learning and school organisation.* San Francisco: Jossey-Bass.

Eraut, M. (1994) *Developing professional knowledge and competence.* London: Routledge.

European Commission (2020) *Communication from the Commission, the European Parliament, the Council, the European Economic and Social Committee and the Committee of the Regions on Achieving the European Education Area by 2025.* Brussels: European Commission.

Eyles, A. and Machin, S. (2015) *Academy schools and their introduction to English education.* London: Centre for Education Economics.

Farrell, C. C., Wentworth, L., and Nayfack, M. (2021) What are the conditions under which research-practice partnerships succeed? *Phi Delta Kappan*, 102(7), 38–41.

Felder, F. (2021) *The ethics of inclusive education. Presenting a new theoretical framework.* London: Routledge.

Fernández-Díaz, E., Calvo, A. and Rodríguez-Hoyos, C. (2014) 'Towards a collaborative action research in Spain to improve teaching practice', *Educational Action Research*, 22(3), pp. 397–410.

Fielding, M., Bragg, S., Craig, J., Cunningham, I., Eraut, M., Gillinson, S., Horne, M., Robinson, C., and Thorp, J. (2005) *Factors influencing the transfer of good practice.* Nottingham: DfES Publications.

Fishman, B.J., Penuel, W.R., Allen, A.R., Cheng, B.H. and Sabelli, N. (2013) 'Design-based implementation research: an emerging model for transforming the relationship of research and practice', *Teachers College*, 115(14), pp. 136–156.

Florian, L. and Black-Hawkins, K. (2011) 'Exploring inclusive pedagogy', *British Educational Research Journal*, 37(5), pp. 813–828.

Forbes, C. (2022). Exploring barriers and solutions to encouraging evidence-into-use within an embedded evaluation approach: reflections from the field. *Review of Education*, 10, e3351. https://doi.org/10.1002/rev3.3351

Forbes, C. and Kerr, K. (2021) Making participation in out-of-school-time provision an asset for young people in high-poverty neighbourhoods. *Educational Review.* https://doi.org/10.1080/00131911.2021.1989380

Freire, P. (1972) *Pedagogy of the oppressed.* London: Penguin.

Fullan, M. (2007) *The new meaning of educational change.* 4th edn. New York: Teachers College Press.

Fullan, M. (2015) *Leadership from the middle: a system strategy. Education Canada* www.cea-ace.ca/educationcanada.

Fullan, M. (2021) *The right drivers for whole system success*. Melbourne: Centre for Strategic Education.

Fullan, M., Rincon-Gallardo, S. and Hargreaves, A. (2015) 'Professional capital as accountability', *Education Policy Analysis Archives*, 23(15). http://dx.doi.org/10.14507/epaa.v23.1998

Galster, G. (2001). On the nature of neighbourhood. *Urban Studies*, 38, pp. 2111–2124. http://dx.doi.org/10.1080/00420980120087072

Gilbert, C. (2018) *Optimism of the will: the development of local area-based education partnerships. A think-piece*. London: UCL Institute of Education.

Giroux, H.A. and Schmidt, M. (2004) 'Closing the achievement gap: a metaphor for children left behind', *Journal of Educational Change*, 5, pp. 213–228.

Grossman, A.S., Lombard, A. and Fisher, N. (2014) *StriveTogether: reinventing the local education ecosystem*. Harvard Business School.

Gutiérrez, K.D. and Penuel, W.R. (2014) 'Relevance to practice as a criterion for rigor', *Educational Researcher*, 43(1), pp. 19–23.

Hadfield, M. and Ainscow, M. (2018) 'Inside a self-improving school system: collaboration, competition and transition', *Journal of Educational Change*, 19(4), pp. 441–462.

Hadfield, M. and Jopling, M. (2018) 'Case study as a means of evaluating the impact of early years leaders: steps, paths and routes', *Evaluation and Program Planning*, 67, pp. 167–176.

Hammersley (2001) 'On 'systematic' reviews of research literatures: a 'narrative' response to Evans & Bene', *British Educational Research Journal*, 27(5), pp. 543–554.

Hargreaves, A. (2023) *Leadership from the middle: the beating heart of educational transformation*. London: Routledge.

Hargreaves, A. and Ainscow, M. (2015) *The top and bottom of leadership and change*. *Phi Delta Kappa*, November, 2015

Hargreaves, A. and Shirley, D. (2020) 'Leading from the middle: its nature, origins and importance', *Journal of Professional Capital and Community*, 5(1), pp. 92–114.

Hargreaves, D.H. (2011) *Leading a self-improving school system*. Nottingham: National College for School Leadership.

Hargreaves, D.H. (1995) 'School culture, school effectiveness and school improvement', *School Effectiveness and School Improvement*, 6(1), pp. 23–27.

Hargreaves, D.H. (2003) Leadership for transformation within the London challenge. Annual Lecture at the London Leadership Centre, 19 May 2003.

Hargreaves, D.H. (2010) *Creating a self-improving school system*. Nottingham: National College for Leadership of Schools and Children's Services.

Hargreaves, D.H. (2010) *Creating a self-improving school system*. Nottingham: National College for School Leadership.

Hargreaves, D.H. (2012a) *A self-improving school system in international context*. Nottingham: National College for School Leadership.

Hargreaves, D.H. (2012b) *A self-improving school system: towards maturity*. Nottingham: National College for School Leadership.

Harris, A., Chapman, C., Muijs, D. and Reynolds, R. (2013) 'Getting lost in translation: the problem of the limited international take-up of educational effectiveness research', *School Leadership and Management*, 33(1), pp. 3–20.

Harris, J., Ainscow, M., Carrington, S. and Kimber, M. (2020) 'Developing inclusive school cultures through ethical practices', in Graham, L.J. (ed.) *Inclusive education in the 21st century: theory, policy and practice*. Sydney: Allen & Unwin.

Harris, J., Carrington, S. and Ainscow, M., with Comber, B., Ehrich, L., Klenowski, V., Smeed, J. and Spina, J. (2017) *Promoting equity in schools: collaboration, inquiry and ethical leadership*. London: Routledge.

Hart, S. (2003) 'Learning without limits', in Nind, M., Sheehy, K. and Simmons, K. (eds.) *Inclusive education: learners and learning contexts*. London: Fulton.

Hart, S., Dixon, A., Drummond, M.J., and McIntyre (2004) *Learning without limits*. Maidenhead: Open University.

Hatch, T., Roegman, R. and Allen, D. (2019) 'Creating equitable outcomes in a segregated state', *Phi Delta Kappan*, 100(5), pp. 19–24.

Hayes, D. (2000) 'Cascade training and teacher professional development', *English Language Teaching Journal*, 54(2), p. 135e145.

Hiebert, J., Gallimore, R. and Stigler, J.W. (2002) 'A knowledge base for the teaching profession: what would it look like and how can we get one?', *Educational Researcher*, 31(5), pp. 3–15.

Hill, H.C., Beisiegel, M. and Jacob, R. (2013) 'Professional development research: consensus, crossroads, and challenges', *Educational Researcher*, 42(9), pp. 476–487.

HM Government (2022) *Levelling up in the United Kingdom*. London: HMSO.

Hopkins, D. (2007) *Every school a great school: realizing the potential of system leadership*. Maidenhead: Open University Press.

Hopkins, D. (2024) *Unleashing greatness: a strategy for school improvement*. Woodbridge: John Catt.

Hopkins, D., Ainscow, M. and West, M. (1994) *School improvement in an era of change*. London: Cassell.

Horn, I.S. and Little, J.W. (2010) 'Attending to problems of practice: routines and resources for professional learning in teachers' workplace interactions', *American Educational Research Journal*, 47(1), pp. 181–217.

Howes, A., Booth, T., Dyson, A. and Frankham, J. (2005) 'Teacher learning and the development of inclusive practices and policies: framing and context', *Research Papers in Education*, 20(2), pp. 133–148.

Howes, A., Frankham, J., Ainscow, M. and Farrell, P. (2004) 'The action in action research: mediating and developing inclusive intentions', *Educational Action Research*, 12(2), pp. 239–258.

REFERENCES

Huberman, M. (1993) 'The model of the independent artisan in teachers' professional relationships' in Little, J. W. and McLaughlin, M. W. (eds.) *Teachers' work: Individuals, colleagues and contexts*. New York, NY: Teachers College Press.

Humes, W. (2020) 'Re-shaping the policy landscape in Scottish education, 2016–20: the limitations of structural reform', *Scottish Educational Review*, 52(2), pp. 89–111.

Husbands, C., Gilbert, C., Gilbert, C., Francis, B. and Wigdortz, B. (2013) *Unleashing greatness: getting the best from an academised system. The report of the academies commission*. London: RSA/Pearson.

Hutchings, M., Hollingworth, S., Mansaray, A., Rose, R. and Greenwood, C. (2012) *Research report DFE-RR215: evaluation of the City challenge programme*. London: Department for Education.

Hutchinson, J., Reader, M. and Akhal, A. (2020) Education in England: Annual Report 2020. Education Policy Institute: London.

Ianes, D., Demo, H. and Dell'Anna, S. (2020) 'Inclusive education in Italy: historical steps, positive developments, and challenges', *Prospects*. https://doi.org/10.1007/s11125-020-09509-7.

Innvaer, S., Vist, G., Trommald, M. and Oxman, A. (2002) 'Health policymakers' perceptions of their use of evidence: a systematic review', *Journal of Health Services Research and Policy*, 7(4), pp. 239–244.

Ishimaru, A. (2022) Transforming the role of RPPs in remaking educational systems. *Educational Researcher*, 51(7), pp. 1–9.

Jaipal, K. and Figg, C. (2011) 'Collaborative action research approaches promoting professional development for elementary school teachers', *Educational Action Research*, 19(1), p. 59e72.

Janis, I. (1982) *Groupthink: pyschological studies of policy decisions*. Houghton Mifflin.

Kerr, K. and Ainscow, M. (2022) 'Promoting equity in market-driven education systems: lessons from England', *Education Science*, 12, p. 495.

Kerr, K. and Ainscow, M. (2023) 'The development of a methodology for enhancing equity within education systems', *International Journal of Research & Method in Education*. https://doi.org/10.1080/1743727X.2023.2231862

Kerr, K., Dyson, A. and Raffo, C. (2014) *Education, disadvantage and place: making the local matter*. Bristol: Policy Press.

Kerr, K. and West, M.(eds.) (2010) *Insight 2: social inequality: can schools narrow the gap?* Macclesfield: British Education Research Association.

Kidson, M. and Norris, E. (2014) *Implementing the London challenge*. London: Joseph Rowntree Foundation.

Kintrea, K. (2021) 'Is there a place for place in educational attainment policy?', *Oxford Review of Education*, 47(2), pp. 207–223.

Ladd, E. and Fiske, H. (2016) Self-governing schools, parental choice, and the need to protect the public interest. Phi Delta Kappan https://kappanonline.org/fiske-ladd-self-governing-schools-parental-choice/

Lamote, C. and Engels, N. (2010) 'The development of student teachers' professional identity', *European Journal of Teacher Education*, 33(1), p. 3e18.

Lefstein, A., Vedder-Weiss, D. and Segal, A. (2020) 'Relocating research on teacher learning: toward pedagogically productive talk', *Educational Researcher*, 49(5), pp. 360–368.

Leithwood, K.A. and Reihl, C. (2003), *What we know about successful leadership*. National College for Educational Leadership. http://dcbsimpson.com/randd-leithwood-successful-leadership.pdf

Levin, B. (2011) 'Mobilising research knowledge in education', *London Review of Education*, 9(1), pp. 15–26.

Lewis, C., Perry, R. and Murata, A. (2006) 'How should research contribute to instructional improvement? The case of lesson study', *Educational Researcher*, 35(3), pp. 3–14.

Lima, J.A. (2008) 'Thinking more deeply about networks in education', *Journal of Educational Change*, 11(1), pp. 1–21.

Lingard, B., Baroutsis, A. and Sellar, S. (2021) 'Enriching educational accountabilities through collaborative public conversations: conceptual and methodological insights from the learning commission approach', *Journal of Educational Change*, 22, pp. 565–587.

Lipman, P. (1997) 'Restructuring in context: a case study of teacher participation and the dynamics of ideology, race and power', *American Educational Research Journal*, 34(1), pp. 3–37.

Locke, T., Alcorn, N. and O'Neill, J. (2013) 'Ethical issues in collaborative action research', *Educational Action Research*, 21, pp. 107–123.

Louis, K.S. (2013) 'Districts, local education authorities, and the context of policy analysis', *Journal of Educational Administration*, 51(4), pp. 550–555.

Lowe, J. (2015) The London schools revolution: something remarkable has happened in the capital's schools. *Prospect*, February 2015.

Madrid Miranda, R. and Chapman, C. (2021) 'Towards a network learning system: reflections on a university initial teacher education and school-based collaborative initiative in Chile', *Professional Development in Education*, 1–15

Mansell, W. (2017) Sixty 'orphan' schools shunned by academy sponsors. *The Guardian*. https://www.theguardian.com/education/2017/feb/07/failing-schools-academy-sponsor-ofsted

Meijer, C.J.W. and Watkins, A. (2019) 'Financing special needs and inclusive education: from Salamanca to the present', *International Journal of Inclusive Education*, 23(7/8), pp. 705–721.

Messiou, K. and Ainscow, M. (2015) 'Engaging with the views of students: a catalyst for powerful teacher development?', *Teacher and Teacher Education Teaching and Teacher Education*, 51(2), pp. 246–255.

Messiou, K. and Ainscow, M. (2020) 'Inclusive inquiry: student-teacher dialogue as a means of promoting inclusion in schools', *British Journal of Educational Research*, 46(3), pp. 670–687.

Messiou, K. and Ainscow, M. (2021) 'Inclusive inquiry: an innovative approach for promoting inclusion in schools', *Revista Latinoamericana Educacion Inclusiva*, 15(2), pp. 23–37.

Messiou, K., Ainscow, M., Echeita, G., Goldrick, S., Hope, M., Paes, I., et al. (2016) 'Learning from differences: a strategy for teacher development in respect to student diversity', *School Effectiveness and School Improvement*, 27(1), pp. 45–61

Messiou, K., Ainscow, M., Galbally, L. and Page, R. (2020) 'Primary school children becoming researchers: the use of inclusive inquiry', *Impact*.

Messiou, K., Bui, L.T.H. and Ainscow, M., et al (2020) 'Student diversity and student voice conceptualisations in five European countries: implications for including all students in schools', *European Educational Research Journal*, 22(2), pp. 355–376

Meyland-Smith, D. and Evans, N. (2009) *A guide to school choice reforms*. London: Policy Exchange.

Mills, T. and Sacrez, A. (2020) 'Could the ideas of T.S', Kuhn Revolutionise Mathematics Teaching? *Australian Mathematics Education Journal*, 2(1), pp. 35–39.

Ministry of Education (2019) *Supporting all schools to succeed: reform of the Tomorrow's schools system*. New Zealand: Ministry of Education.

Mitton, C., Adair, C.E., McKenzie, E., Patten, S.B. and Perry, B.W. (2007) 'Knowledge transfer and exchange: review and synthesis of the literature', *Milbank Quarterly*, 85(4), pp. 729–768.

Mourshed, M., Chijioke, C. and Barber, M. (2010) *How the world's most improved school systems keep getting better*. London: McKinsey & Company.

Muijs, D., Ainscow, M., Chapman, C. and West, M. (2011) *Collaboration and networking in education*. London: Springer.

Muijs, D. and Rumyantseva, N. (2014) 'Coopetition in education: collaborating in a competitive environment', *Journal of Educational Change*, 15(1), pp. 1–18.

Mulford, B. (2007) 'Building social capital in professional learning communities: importance, challenges and a way forward', in Stoll and Seashore Louis, K. (eds.) *Professional learning communities: divergence, depth and dilemmas*. London: Open University Press.

OECD (2010), *PISA 2009 results: Overcoming social background – Equity in learning opportunities and outcomes (Volume II)*. Paris: OECD

OECD (2012) *Equity and quality in education: supporting disadvantaged students and schools*. Paris: OECD Publishing.

OECD (2018) *Education at a glance 2018: OECD indicators*. Paris: OECD Publishing.

OECD (2021) *Education at a glance 2021: OECD indicators*. Paris: OECD Publishing.

OECD (2022) *Review of inclusive education in Portugal*. Paris: OECD Publishing.

REFERENCES

Ofsted (2019) Off-rolling: exploring the issue. Gov UK https://www.gov.uk/government/publications/off-rolling-exploring-the-issue

Opertti, R., Walker, Z. and Zhang, Y. (2014) Inclusive education: from targeting groups and schools to achieving quality education as the core of EFA, in Florian, L.(ed.) *The SAGE handbook of special education* (2nd Revised edn). London: SAGE.

Opfer, V.D. and Pedder, D. (2010) 'Benefits, status and effectiveness of continuous professional development for teachers in England', *Curriculum Journal*, 21(4), p. 413e431.

Pampaka, M., Williams, J. and Homer, M. (2016) 'Is the educational 'what works' agenda working? Critical methodological developments', *International Journal of Research & Method in Education*, 39(3), pp. 231–236.

Payne., C.M. (2008) *So much reform, so little change: the persistence of failure in urban schools*. Cambridge: Harvard Education Press.

Penuel, W.R., Coburn, C.E. and Gallagher, D. (2013) 'Negotiating problems of practice in research-practice partnerships focused on design', in Fishman, B.J., Penuel, W.R., Allen, A.-R. and Cheng B. H. (eds.), *Design-based implementation research: Theories, methods, and exemplars. National Society for the Study of Education Yearbook*. New York: Teachers College Record, pp. 237–255

Penuel, W.R., Riedy, R., Barber, M.S., Peurach, D.J., LeBouef, W.A. and Clark, T. (2020) 'Principles of collaborative education research with stakeholders: toward requirements for a new research and development infrastructure', *Review of Educational Research*, 90(5), pp. 627–674.

Pickett, K. and Vanderbloemen, L. (2015) *Mind the gap: tackling social and educational inequality*. New York: Cambridge Primary Review Trust.

Preston, et al (2012) 'School innovation in district context: comparing traditional public schools and charter schools,' *Economics of Education Review*, 31(2) 318–330

Reay, D. (2022) 'Lessons from abroad: how can we achieve a socially just educational system?, *Irish Educational Studies*, 41(3), pp. 425–440.

Reimers, F. and McGinn, N. (1997) *Informed dialogue: using research to shape education policy around the world*. Westport: Noel Greenwood Publishing.

Reynolds, D. (1991) 'Changing ineffective schools', in Ainscow, M. (ed.) *Effective schools for all* (pp. 92–105). London: Fulton.

Riehl, C.J. (2000) 'The principal's role in creating inclusive schools for diverse students: a review of normative, empirical, and critical literature on the practice of educational administration', *Review of Educational Research*, 70(1), pp. 55–81.

Robinson, V., Lloyd, C. and Rowe, K. (2008) 'The impact of leadership on student outcomes: an analysis of the differential effects of leadership types', *Educational Administration Quarterly*, 44(5), pp. 635–674.

Rosenholtz, S.J. (1989) *Teachers' workplace: the social organization of schools*. New York: Longman.

REFERENCES

Sabel, C., Saxenian, A., Miettinen, R., Kristenson, P.H. and Hautamaki, J. (2011) *Individualized service provision in the new welfare state: lessons from special education in Finland.* Helsinki: SITRA.

Safstrom, C.A. and Mansson, N. (2022) 'The marketisation of education and the democratic deficit', *European Educational Research Journal*, 21(1), pp. 124–137.

Salokangas, M. and Ainscow, M. (2017) *Inside the autonomous school: making sense of a global educational trend.* London: Routledge.

Sammons, P., Lindorff, A., Ortega, L. and Kington, A. (2016) 'Inspiring teaching: learning from exemplary practitioners', *Journal of Professional Capital & Community*, 1(2), pp. 124–144.

Sarason, S.B. (1990) *The predictable failure of educational reform: can we change course Before it's too late?* San Francisco, CA: Jossey-Bass.

Schein, E. (1985) *Organisational culture and leadership.* San Francisco: Jossey-Bass.

Schildkamp, K., Ehren, M. and Kuin Lai, M.K. (2012) 'Editorial article for the special issue on data-based decision making around the world: from policy to practice to results', *School Effectiveness and School Improvement*, 23(2), pp. 123–131.

Schleicher, A. (2010) 'International comparisons of student learning outcomes', in Hargreaves, A., Lieberman, A., Fullan, M. and Hopkins, D. (eds.) *Second handbook of educational change.* London: Springer.

Schön, D. (2017) *The reflective practitioner: how professionals think in action.* London: Taylor and Francis.

Sharples, J., Maxwell, B. and Coldwell, M. (2023) 'Developing a systems-based approach to research use in education', *BERA Blog*, 13th February 2023. Available at https://www.bera.ac.uk/blog/developing-a-systems-based-approach-to-research-use-in-education

Sjölund, S., Lindvall, J., Larsson, M. and Ryve, A. (2022) 'Mapping roles in research-practice partnerships–a systematic literature review', *Educational Review*, 2, 1–29.

Skrtic, T.M. (1991) 'The special education paradox: equity as the way to excellence', *Harvard Educational Review*, 61(2), pp. 148–206.

Smith, K. (1999) *Beyond evidence-based policy in public health: the interplay of ideas.* Basingstoke: Palgrave Macmillan.

Spillane, J. P., Seelig, J. L., Blaushild, N. L., Cohen, D. K., and Peurach, D. J. (2019) Educational system building in a changing educational sector: Environment, organization and the technical core. *Educational Policy*, 33(6), pp. 846–881.

Spina, N., Harris, J., Carrington, S. and Ainscow, M. (2019) 'Resisting governance by numbers', in Riddle, S., and Apple, M.W. (eds.) *Re-imagining education for democracy.* London: Routledge.

Sullivan, H. and Skelcher, C. (2002) *Collaborating across boundaries.* London: Palgrave.

Talbert, J.E. and McLaughlin, M. (2002) 'Professional communities and the artisan model of teaching', *Teachers and Teaching: theory and Practice*, 8(3/4), pp. 325–343.

Tervasmäki, T., Okkolin, M.-A. and Kauppinen, I. (2020) 'Changing the heart and soul? Inequalities in Finland's current pursuit of a narrow education policy', *Policy Futures in Education*, 18(5), pp. 648–661.

Tinoca, L., Piedade, J., Santos, S., Pedro, A., and Gomes, S. (2022) Design-based research in the educational field: a systematic literature review. *Education Sciences*, 12(6), 410. https://doi.org/10.3390/educsci12060410.

UIS. (2019) *Fact Sheet No. 56*. Paris: UNESCO http://uis.unesco.org/sites/default/files/documents/new-methodology-shows-258-million-children-adolescents-and-youth-are-out-school.pdf

UNESCO (2015) *Education for all 2000–2015: achievements and challenges*. Paris: UNESCO.

UNESCO (2017) *Ensuring inclusion and equity in education*. Paris: UNESCO.

UNESCO (2020) *Global education monitoring report 2020 – Latin America and the Caribbean – inclusion and education: all means all*. Paris: UNESCO.

UNICEF (2018) *An unfair start: inequality in children's education in rich countries*, Innocenti Report Card 15. Florence: UNICEF Office of Research – Innocenti.

Vaino, K., Holbrook, J. and Rannikmäe, M. (2013) 'A case study examining change in teacher beliefs through collaborative action research', *International Journal of Science Education*, 35(1), pp. 1–30.

Varjo, J. and Kalalahti, M. (2019) 'The art of governing local education markets – municipalities and school choice in Finland', *Education Inquiry*, 10(2), pp. 151–165.

Weick, K.E. (1985) 'Sources of order in underorganised systems: themes in recent organisational theory', in Lincoln, Y.S. (ed.) *Organisational theory and inquiry*. Beverley Hills: Sage.

Wenger, E. (1998) *Communities of practice: learning, meaning and identity*. Cambridge: Cambridge University Press.

West, M. and Ainscow, M. (2010) 'Improving schools in Hong Kong: a description of the improvement model and some reflections on its impact on schools, teachers and school principals', in Huber, S. (ed.) *School leadership – international perspectives*. London: Springer.

West, M., Ainscow, M. and Nottman, H. (2003) *What leaders read: key texts from education and beyond*. Nottingham: National College for School Leadership.

Whitehurst, G.J. and Croft, M. (2010) *The Harlem Children's zone, promise neighborhoods, and the broader, bolder approach to education*. Washington: The Brookings Institution.

Whitty, G. (2006) Education(al) research and education policy making: Is conflict inevitable?, *British Educational Research Journal*, 32(2), pp. 159–176.

Wilkinson, R. and Pickett, K. (2000) *The spirit level*. London: Allen Lane.

Yost, D.S., Sentner, S.M. and Forlenza-Bailey, A. (2000) 'An examination of the construct of critical reflection: implications for teacher education programming in the 21st century', *Journal of Teacher Education*, 51(1), pp. 39–49.

YouGov (2019) Exploring the issue of off-rolling. On behalf of Ofsted. https://assets.publishing.service.gov.uk/government/uploads/system/uploads/attachment_data/file/936524/Ofsted_offrolling_report_YouGov_090519.pdf

Yurkofsky, M.M., Peterson, A.J., et al (2020) 'Research on continuous improvement: exploring the complexities of managing educational change. *review of research i*agenda', in Florian, L. (ed.) *The Sage handbook of special education*, 2nd edn. London: Sage

Index

Note: Page numbers in *italics* refer to figures/illustrations.

academies: in England 8, 84, 92, 107, 113, 115, 138; programme 83–84, 107; state-funded schools 107
accountability educational systems 32–33, 141
action-oriented approaches 112
administrators 30–31
Ainscow, M. 16, 19
anxieties 47, 73
area-based collaboration 31
Argyris, C. 151
Armstrong, P. 85
artisanship 61
Askell-Williams, H. 144
assessment: forms of 4; processes 141
asset-based approaches 103
austerity 109
autism spectrum disorders 73
Avalos, B. 59

Bales, R. 50–51
Barrenechea, I. 145
Beech, J. 145
behavioural challenges 73
Beisiegel, M. 60
between-school factors 22
beyond-school factors *see* outside-school factors

Black-Hawkins, K. 62
Booth, T. 13
bottom-up leadership 48–49, 158
Burgess, S. 40

Calderon, I 71, 80
Central South Wales (CSW) region 22, 46–48
Challenge programmes 32–56
Chapman, C. 144
charter schools in the USA 8
Checkland, P. 144, 165
Children's Neighbourhoods Scotland initiative 102
City Challenge in England 22, 43–47, 89, 132
city-wide partnership 88
coaching 129
collaborative alliance with local education authority 67
collaborative forms of professional learning 66; analysis of contexts 66; building on existing practices 66; clarity of meaning 66; evaluating progress 67; managing change 67; working collaboratively 66
collaborative participation 60
collaborative professional learning 70

community-based programmes 29
community-focused arrangements 103
community of practice 59, 77
competition between schools 104
conception of diversity 69
conscience of the system 98
contextual barriers 65, 79, 140–141, 148
contextually astute 12
coopetition 97
co-ordination of system 48
COVID pandemic 83, 147, 152, 154, 159
curriculum 141
Curriculum for Excellence 147

degree of risk taking 64
design-based equity research 111, 163
design-based implementation research 148–149
development of routines 78
disability discrimination 5
Dobbie, W. 102
doubly holistic 102
Dundee initiative 144–146, 154–155, 158
Dyson, A. 162

easy-to-recall formulations 43
ecology of equity 21
Edison, T. 140
EDLM *see* Every Dundee Learner Matters
education(al): change 17; equity 9, 15, 24; improvement 140; inequalities 7; inequities 3; market-place 87; policy panoply 115; reforms 58; standardization 34; *see also* system reform initiatives
Education Commission 136
education departments 30–31
Education for All (EFA) movement 1–2; context 12–14; current situation 3–4; developments 4–7; global trends 8–9; influencing policy-making 11–12; research and policy-making 9–10
Education 2030 Framework for Action 3
education systems 10; decision-making regarding 51; development of 2, 101; feature of 89; reforming 142
EFA Declaration 1
Elmore, R. 58
English education landscape 84
English national policy for education 130

equitable educational arrangements 113
equity in education systems 3–4, 9, 15, 38; barriers to progress 48–56; challenges 91–94; Greater Manchester Challenge 41–44; London Challenge 39–41; National Initiative in Wales 44–46; Regional Challenge 46–48; United Kingdom 3, 38–39
Equity Research Network 20
Eraut, M 78
Ethical Leadership 20
ethics of care 80
European Commission 3
European Union 7
Every Child Matters 39
Every Dundee Learner Matters (EDLM) 146–147, 158; barriers 158–160; collaborative action research 152–154; design features *150*, 150–152; developing inclusive cultures 156–158; engaging with evidences 154–156; organisational cultures 160–161; participation 151; presence 151; progress 151; strategy 147–150
Every learner matters and matters equally (UNESCO) 141
evidence-based interventions 100
evidence-based policy-making 11
evidence-based professional learning 58–59
Evidence for Policy and Practice Information Coordinating Centre 55
external accountability 32
Eyles, A. 84

faith schools 113
families and community partners 143
Families of Schools 42, 88
Fielding, M. 60
Fishman, B.J. 148
Fiske, H. 107
Florek, A. 85
Florian, L. 62
freedom of school leaders 54
free schools in Sweden 8
Fryer, R.G. 102
Fullan, M. 32, 105, 120, 123, 154
funding 141

GCSE examinations 48, 131
Gilbert, C. 85, 94
Global Monitoring Report 3
government-driven priorities 93

INDEX

government-instigated improvement initiatives 121
Greater Manchester Challenge 41–44, 121
groupthink 61, 147

Hammersley 55
Hargreaves, A. 34–36, 98, 122
Hargreaves, D. 61, 64, 76
Harlem Children's Zone 102
Harris, A. 11
Hart, S. 62
Hayes, D. 60
headteacher strategy group 135
high-performing education system 147
Hill, H.C. 60
Hopkins, D. 17, 36
Howes, A. 22
Hughes, B. 85
humanise educational relationships 80
Humes, W. 147, 160

IBE-UNESCO International Conference on Education, 2008 2
implementation 154
Improving the Quality of Education for All (IQEA) 17
inadequate teacher preparation and support 4
inappropriate curricula 4
inclusion and equity in education 3–4, 7–8, 25–26, 36, 65, 80, 140; contextual analysis 25; family involvement 29; inform all educational policies 141; as principles 26–28; progress in relation to 141–142; promotion of 30; wider community involvement 29–30
inclusive cultures 156–158; innovation 157; inquiring stance 157
inclusive education 15; in Canada 5, 7; elements of 5; in Finland 6; movement towards 2–3; policy 5; in Portugal 5–6; Sierra Leone 5; in Vietnam 6
Inclusive Education Act of 2018 23
inclusive pedagogical approach 62
inclusive pedagogy 62
inclusive practices 28, 58; barriers 70–73; challenges 75–76; changing school cultures 76–77; collaboration 59–61; developing inclusive practices 61–63; focusing on 67–70; leading school developments 79–81; Leaving No One behind 73–75; nature of practice 78–79; resources 64–67; teacher development 58–59; using evidence 63–64
inclusive school 72; development 28–29; development with teacher 19
independent state schools 84–85
Index for Inclusion 18–19; *Equity Research Network* 20; *Ethical Leadership* 20; Inclusive Inquiry 20; *Promoting inclusion and equity in Latin America* 21; *Reaching Out to All Learners* 20–21; *Understanding and Developing Inclusive Practices in Schools* 19–20
inequalities 38, 105
initiation 154
institutionalisation 154

Jacob, R. 60
Janis, I. 61
joint practice development 60

Kerr, K. 112
Keys to Success schools 42, 125–126
Khochen-Bagshaw, M. 23
Kidson, M. 40
Kintrea, K. 160
knowledge: generation 112, 145; mobilisation 11–12
Koh, G.A. 144
KS3 subject specialist vocabulary 117

Ladd, E. 107
large-scale system 51
Latvia 7
Laws, D. 12
leadership 123; for equitable developments 118
learning: commissions 103; communities 81
learning of students: between-school factors 22; beyond-school factors 22; within-school factors 22
Learning without Limits 62
Leaving No One behind 73–75
Lefstein, A. 63
'levelling up' strategy 119
Levin, B. 11
Lima, J.A. 100
Lingard, B. 103
Lipman, P. 61
Lithuania 7
local area level, inclusion and equity 143–144; addressing obstacles 130–131; collaboration 136–138;

INDEX

crossing borders 126–127; keys to success 124–126; middle tier 121–123; supporting improvements 127–129; support strategies 123–124; team work 129–130
local authorities 128; relationships with 93
local-coordinated partnerships 94
local coordination 31
London Challenge 39–41
London effect 38
long-term collaboration 148
Louis, K. S. 130
Lowe, J. 40

Machin, S. 84
maintained schools 113
Mansell, W. 110
market-driven approach to educational policies 106
MATs *see* multi-academy trusts
McGinn, N. 10
McLaughlin, M. 61
mediating layer 122
middle class parents 91
middle-level administrative structure 121
middle tier arrangements 53
Morley, A. 127
Muijs, D. 105
multi-academy trusts (MATs) 84, 92, 99, 107, 109, 114–115, 118, 131–132, 135, 137
multi-agency support 81
Muncey, J. 16

national curriculum 84
national education systems 11
National Health Service 116
National Initiative in Wales 44–46
national-level standardised attainment tests 107
national policy in England 97
National Policy on Radical Inclusion in schools 5
networkers 11
New Zealand 8
Norris, E. 40

off-rolling 109
Ofsted 40, 108, 135
Opfer, V.D. 59
organisational flexibility within schools 59

Organisation for Economic Co-operation and Development 7
orphan schools 110
outside-school factors 22, 101; analysing developments 110–119; challenges 105–109; community involvement 102–103; equitable practices 112–113; impacts 109–110; local alliances 113–114; market forces, impact of 103–105; redefining relationships 114–116; third-sector organisations 116–117

partnerships between schools 82–83, 142–143; availability of resources 93; challenges 91–94; contexts 88–89; developments 85–86, 97–98; English context 83; features 88–91; future 96–99; implication 94–95; independent state schools 84–85; individuals 90; lack of mandate 94; lessons from the field 87–88; local authorities 93; market forces 86–87; peer inquiry 95–96; relationships 89–90; school diversity 92; use of evidence 91; values 90–91; *see also* collaborative alliance with local education authority; Families of Schools
Pathways to Success 45–46
Pedder, D. 59
peer inquiry 95–96
Penuel, W.R. 148
place-based initiatives 102–103
place-based partnerships 130, 143
place-based school-to-school collaboration 117
policy change in education 11
policy entrepreneurs 90
political bureaucracy 35
Portuguese education system 5–6, 23–25
Poulter, J. 165
poverty-related attainment gap 147
problem-solvers 12
problem-solving function 76
professional development 21, 58–60; activities 80; for teachers 16
professional hour 129
Programme for International Student Assessment (PISA) 6, 25, 32
Promoting inclusion and equity in Latin America 21

INDEX

radical paradigm shift 105
Rayner, S. 85
Reaching Out to All Learners 20–21
reality-defining function of culture 76
Reay, D. 98
Regional Challenge 46–48
Reimers, F. 10
Report Card (UNICEF) 7
research-practice partnerships 148, 164–165
Reynolds, D. 155
Riedy, R. 148
Rivas, A. 145
Robert Bales' theory of group systems 50–51
Robinson, V. 80
Rumyantseva, N. 105

Schein, E. 76
Schon, D. 151
school-based expertise 93
school-based staff development activities 18
school development 16, 81
school improvement partnership (SIP) 155
school improvement with attitude 19
school leaders 28–29, 87, 132, 143
school-led improvement 143
school partnerships *see* partnerships between schools
schools: autonomous 104; autonomy 107; coordinators, training for 18; diversity 92; governance 104; learning communities 142; quality assurance systems 104–105
Schools Challenge Cymru in Wales 22, 44–46, 121
school-to-school collaboration 31, 139, 142
Scottish Attainment Challenge 49
Scottish education policies 146–147
Segal, A. 63
self-improving schools 33–34, 81; development of 36; *First Way* 34; *Fourth Way* 34–36; *Second Way* 34; *Third Way* 34
self-managing 12
sense of 'togetherness' 137
Shirley, D. 34, 123
Skelcher, C. 11
skilled communicators 11
Smith, K. 119

SNAP *see* Special Needs Action Programme
social capital 61, 89
social exclusion 79
socialising challenges 73
social network analysis surveys 154
Special Needs Action Programme (SNAP) 16; primary schools 16–17; secondary sector 16–17; Small Steps 16; staff development package 16–17; *working with, rather than working on* 18
Staff College 85
staff development packages 16
strategic decision-making 86
strategic in orientation 12
StriveTogether 102
student having special needs 80
Sullivan, H. 11
sustainability 53
Sustainable Development Goals (SDGs) 3; 4 – *ensure inclusive and equitable quality education for all* 3
system leaders 36, 90
system reform initiatives 48; cultural factors 49, 53–55; political factors 49, 51–53; social factors 49–51
system-wide reform development 140

Talbert, J.E. 61
teachers: education 141; pay 84; professional development 58–60; professionalism 35; routines 78
Teach First 40
teaching schools 43
think pieces 36
third-sector organisations 116–117
three As *(Aspirations, Access,* and *Achieve)* 43
Transforming Secondary Education 22
transparency 32
trios of teachers 68–70

Understanding and Developing Inclusive Practices in Schools 19–20
UNESCO 73; *Guide for Ensuring Inclusion and Equity in Education* 4
UNESCO-IBE 20
UNESCO Institute for Statistics data 3
UNESCO-International Bureau of Education 65
UNICEF 3

Vedder-Weiss, D. 63
Viola, M. 73

Wales 22–23, 44–45, 51, 53, 127, 135
Welsh initiative 45
Wenger, E. 59, 76–77, 80
Whitty, G. 10
within-school factors 22

within-school strategies 82
World Conference on Special Needs Education, 1994 2
World Education Forum meeting, 2000 2

Yurkofsky, M.M. 149

For Product Safety Concerns and Information please contact our EU
representative GPSR@taylorandfrancis.com
Taylor & Francis Verlag GmbH, Kaufingerstraße 24, 80331 München, Germany

www.ingramcontent.com/pod-product-compliance
Lightning Source LLC
Chambersburg PA
CBHW070309230426
43664CB00015B/2690